LET IT BE /
ABBEY ROAD

160020

	DATE DUE		

CLASSIC ROCK ALBUMS
Series Editor: Clinton Heylin

LET IT BE / ABBEY ROAD

THE BEATLES

Peter Doggett

SCHIRMER BOOKS
An Imprint of Simon & Schuster Macmillan
New York

Prentice Hall International
London   Mexico City   New Delhi   Singapore   Sydney   Toronto

The author and publisher are grateful for permission to quote from the following:

"Abbey Road" by John Mendelssohn and Ed Ward, from *Rolling Stone*, November 15, 1969, by Straight Arrow Publishers, Inc., 1969. All rights reserved Reprinted by permission.
"Let It Be" by John Mendelssohn, from *Rolling Stone*, June 11, 1970, by Straight Arrow Publishers, Inc., 1970. All rights reserved. Reprinted by permission.
"Those Inventive Beatles" and "Strong As Ever" by William Mann © Times Newspapers Limited 1969 and 1970, © Times Newspapers Limited 1998.
"New LP Shows They Couldn't Care Less" by Alan Smith © IPC Magazines Limited 1970. All rights reserved.

Schirmer Books
An Imprint of Simon & Schuster Macmillan
1633 Broadway
New York, NY 10019

Library of Congress Catalog Card Number: 97–29051

Printed in the United States of America

Printing Number
10 9 8 7 6 5 4 3 2 1

Library of Congress Cataloging-in-Publication Data

Doggett, Peter.
  Let it be/Abbey Road : The Beatles / Peter Doggett.
    p. cm. — (Classic rock albums)
  ISBN 0–02–864772–6 (alk. paper)
    1. Beatles. Let it be. 2. Beatles. Abbey Road. 3. Rock music—
  History and criticism. I. Title. II. Series.
  ML421.B4D64 1998   97–29051
  782.42166'0922—dc21   CIP
                                                               MN

This paper meets the requirements of ANSI/NISO Z.39.48–1992 (Permanence of Paper).

CONTENTS

To
Doug Sulpy
and
Ray Schweighardt
in awe of their
pioneering research

LET IT BE /
ABBEY ROAD

THE BEATLES

THE ALBUMS

FUTURE GENERATIONS, VAGUE ON
THE CHRONOLOGY OF EVENTS, WILL FIND IT HARD TO DISCERN
THE DISHARMONY OF THAT ENVIRONMENT IN WHICH SO MUCH
MARVELLOUS MUSIC WAS CREATED.

Derek Taylor, *Fifty Years Adrift*

"Genius is pain," proclaimed John Lennon in 1970. It was an equation that the Beatles had already tested to its limits.

They began 1969 with a simple target: to perform in public for the first time in three years, and to document the event for posterity. They set aside the month of January for this purpose, assuming that they'd then be free to indulge in another laborious series of recording sessions—of the kind that had spawned previous studio epics like *Sgt. Pepper* and *The Beatles* (aka *The White Album*).

The live concert duly took place, albeit without an audience. It formed the climax of a documentary film about the making of a Beatles record, and the resulting soundtrack LP won both an Oscar and a Grammy. After a suitable pause, the quartet began work on a studio project, *Abbey Road,* which became the best-selling album of their career. But this résumé of success masks one inescapable fact: the process of completing—or in one case refusing to complete—those two albums ended up destroying the Beatles.

As the group's publicist, Derek Taylor was more aware than most of the internal conflict that scarred the quartet that year. It was his sorry task

The Apple rooftop, January 30, 1969.
COURTESY OF PHOTOFEST

1

to compose snippets of corporate optimism about their magical powers, while all around him their Apple Corps offices shook to the rhythms of fragmentation. Even so, Taylor considered one aspect of their lives unsullied by the bloodletting of 1969. "Ignore all other versions of this truth," he wrote in his autobiography. "The Beatles never debauched their art in the studio."

The aural evidence suggests otherwise. In January 1969, Lennon, McCartney, Harrison, and Starkey devoted four weeks to debauching their art, their music, their camaraderie, their reputations, their existence as a unit. They emerged with nothing that resembled a professional album, and only the need in 1970 to concoct a soundtrack record for the long-promised documentary movie persuaded them to turn over the wreckage of those sessions to an outside producer, Phil Spector.

By that time, the Beatles were no longer a unit in anything but name. They had effectively collapsed the previous summer, when weeks of futile business wranglings fueled the lingering discontent between John Lennon and Paul McCartney. The former songwriting partners agreed to bury their differences for as long as it took to complete *Abbey Road* in the summer of 1969. Then Lennon informed his colleagues that he was leaving the group. Seven months before the news became public, the Beatles ceased to exist.

Somehow, operating on instinct, the Beatles managed to create even as they were decaying from within. As the raw film and audio footage from January 1969 reveals, music was sometimes the trigger for the group's disharmony, sometimes the antidote. Thereafter, the Beatles fell back on craftsmanship and sleight of hand—employing magic tricks so convincing that they sometimes forgot that their decade-long friendship had soured.

The ultimate irony is this: little in pop history glows with the melodic freedom and glitzy self-confidence of *Abbey Road.* Indeed, two of the group, and their producer, continue to rate it as the Beatles' finest work. Even in the midst of chaos, the group couldn't help but make music that would survive as a symbol of the utopian ideals of the '60s.

Let It Be and *Abbey Road* are indissolubly linked. In a narrative sense, *Let It Be* was recorded before *Abbey Road,* but assembled and released after it. Moreover, almost all the songs on *Abbey Road* were unveiled, in varying stages of completion, during the January 1969 sessions that produced *Let It Be.* Those unhappy weeks at Twickenham Film Studios and then at Apple's Savile Row headquarters were preserved for posterity on tape in unprecedented detail. If this book concentrates on the bitterness and pain of those sessions at the expense of the smoother, less dramatic birth of *Abbey Road,* that's because the events of January 1969 ensured the group's fate.

Ultimately, the two albums are two halves of one tale, two responses to one fact. During 1969, the Beatles fell apart. *Let It Be* documented the month when the group realized that their demise was inevitable; *Abbey Road* was their attempt to erect a respectable tombstone. Together, the albums' creation and completion provide a compelling finale to an irresistible process of disintegration which had first become apparent a year earlier during the relentless sessions for *The White Album.*

The White Album had taken five months to record in 1968, providing ample opportunity for the group's internal dynamics to uncoil in unexpected directions. Ringo Starr remembered that during the summer-long sessions "we never really argued in the studio. That was the funny thing. We always sort of held back a bit. Maybe if we'd argued a lot more, then it wouldn't have got to the stage it got to." But his judgment is undermined by the testimony of other observers, who noted a subtle shift in the quartet's relations from tension to antagonism.

By mid-July 1968, the atmosphere in the studio had soured to the point that the Beatles' longtime engineer, Geoff Emerick, requested leave of absence from the sessions. "I lost interest in the *White Album* because they were really arguing amongst themselves and swearing at each other," he told Mark Lewisohn. "The expletives were really flying. I went down to the studio to explain it to the group and John Lennon said, 'Look, we're not moaning and getting uptight about you, we're complaining about EMI. Why can't they decorate it?' Admittedly the studio did need smartening up a little bit, but I knew this was just an outlet for a bigger problem. They were falling apart."

A month later, George Harrison abruptly announced that he was taking his wife to Greece for the weekend and that the others could carry on without him. On his return, Ringo Starr quit the group. True to his media caricature as the silent, sad-eyed drummer, he didn't harangue the others; he simply announced he was leaving and drove home to his gadget-strewn mansion in the Surrey stockbroker belt.

Placated by a telegram from Lennon, Starr returned after two weeks, in time for the Beatles to film performances of their new single, "Hey Jude"/"Revolution," for TV's *David Frost Show*. It was their first appearance before an audience in more than two years, and McCartney, a natural showman, relished the interaction with his public. As they played "Hey Jude," director Michael Lindsay-Hogg encouraged the audience to mingle with the stars, and the TV cameras caught a rare moment when the barriers between public and performers were pulled aside. Sensing the democracy of the moment, Lennon turned his microphone toward the fans, while McCartney launched into an adrenaline-fueled series of whoops and screams, like an animal suddenly restored to its natural habitat.

The collective energy and elation of that performance survived into the next set of studio sessions. Tentatively, McCartney began to suggest that the Beatles should consider the possibility of playing live concerts again. For once, none of the others balked at the idea.

In August 1966, the Beatles had played their last official live concert, at Candlestick Park in San Francisco. It was the culmination of three years of frenetic touring, which had sapped their energies to the limit. During their final worldwide jaunt in the summer of '66, they'd been threatened with death by religious zealots in the United States and left the Philippines in fear of President Marcos's security forces. Only too aware that they'd become a traveling freak show, inaudible above the frenzied screams of their fans, the group opted to continue their career within the altogether safer confines of Abbey Road studios in London.

The death of Beatles manager Brian Epstein in August 1967 removed the only figure who could have persuaded them to return to the road. In his absence, Paul McCartney became the group's self-appointed cheerleader. Though Lennon subsequently claimed that he had resented the way in which his partner "bounced" the Beatles into project after project in the late '60s, it's clear that if he had been in control of their destiny, there would have been no *Magical Mystery Tour,* no *White Album,* and certainly no *Abbey Road* or *Let It Be.* McCartney's enthusiasm may have seemed intrusive to the ever more unfocused Lennon, but without it the Beatles might just as well have died with Epstein.

Having taken virtual control of the group's newly launched Apple Corps, a multimedia attempt to subvert capitalism in the interests of art and free expression, McCartney can have felt little compunction about attempting to steer the Beatles' career along a course of his own design. In late September 1968, Apple executives made a provisional booking at London's most prestigious concert hall, the Royal Albert Hall, for an unspecified date in December. A week later, Apple announced that the Beatles would be performing at the venue before Christmas, supported by labelmates like Mary Hopkin and James Taylor. However, the Albert Hall booking was canceled when McCartney realized that the Beatles would need several days at the venue just to acclimate themselves to live performance. Instead, Apple opted for the Roundhouse, a bastion of late '60s underground rock, in London's Chalk Farm district. The circular theater had already played host to residencies by psychedelic pioneers like Pink Floyd. By shifting from the opulence of the Albert Hall, the Beatles (or at least McCartney) were symbolically opting for the counterculture. "What's probable," McCartney hinted to the *New Musical Express* at the start of October, "is that before we do anything else, we will do our own TV show in which we'll perform the numbers from the new album." But he had to admit that the other members of the group had not as yet agreed to take part in the show.

For the moment, the proposal was set aside, as a series of mammoth sessions were staged to complete *The White Album*. Ringo Starr left for a fortnight's holiday on 14 October; two days later, George Harrison set off for Los Angeles, where he was due to produce an album for Apple artist Jackie Lomax. In their absence, Lennon and McCartney briefly rekindled some old camaraderie. For twenty-four hours, the pair supervised the final mixing and assembly of the thirty-track double album, emerging late on the afternoon of 17 October with the Beatles' longest, most eclectic, and arguably most inspired record.

The following morning, the central London flat owned by Ringo Starr, currently the residence of John Lennon and his girlfriend Yoko Ono, was raided by the Metropolitan Police, who "discovered" quantities of cannabis resin. "Imagine your worst paranoia, because it's here," Lennon told Apple's Neil Aspinall as Detective-Sergeant Pilcher and his narcotics squad—human and canine—rooted through the jumble of clothes and artwork in his bedroom.

Among the artifacts the police examined were the blown-up photographs of a nude Lennon and Ono intended for the cover of the couple's first joint album, *Unfinished Music No. 1: Two Virgins.* Taped on 20 May 1968, shortly before they made love for the first time, *Two Virgins* was an erratic avant-garde concoction, a rich man's plaything coated in the veneer of experimental art. It would have aroused little interest without its stark, not to say stomach-turning, artwork. "If you must have a naked man on the cover," asked EMI boss Sir Joseph Lockwood when Lennon presented him with the photos, "why didn't you use Paul instead?"

Ostensibly McCartney lent the starry-eyed lovers his full support. "When two saints meet, it is a humbling experience," he wrote on the album sleeve. But behind the scenes, he sided with those encouraging Lennon to abandon the project.

His paranoia increased by the drug bust, Lennon regarded McCartney's backstage maneuvering as a betrayal. Early in November, he taped a none-too-cryptic "poem" for inclusion on the Beatles' annual Christmas giveaway to their fans. "Jock and Yono" related the bitter experiences of "two balloons . . . strictly in love-bound to happen in a million years." Beset by universal opposition, "they battled on against overwhelming oddities, includo some of there beast friends."

"They went on and on," Lennon remarked later of his fellow Beatles, "just being abusive and trying to pretend that Yoko didn't exist, and that she didn't have any art, that she had a lucky break meeting me, and that she should be on her fucking knees, and not interfere with them. But she stood up to them: she'd start telling them, as an equal, what she thought about any given situation. And they couldn't take it" *(John Lennon: For the Record).*

Vilified in the press—for being, in order, Japanese, an artist with unusual tastes, and a married woman—Yoko Ono was also the subject of a resentment that bordered on hostility from the other Beatles and their aides. The "girls" had always been unofficially barred from watching their men at work, but Lennon shattered this unwritten rule during the *White Album* sessions by insisting that Yoko sit beside him throughout. Her presence undoubtedly hindered the free flow of ideas and invective among the erstwhile Fab Four.

While Lennon and Ono were undergoing trial by media, Paul McCartney was also becoming entangled in matters of the heart. In November 1968, the American photographer Linda Eastman moved into his London home, the culmination of an affair that had begun in New

York earlier that year. For the moment, the arrival of this "leggy blonde beauty," as the British press described her, had little effect on the Beatles. But the fact that she was the daughter and sister of a pair of show-business lawyers would soon create unforeseen complications in McCartney's life.

The balance of power within the Beatles was still weighted in Paul's favor at the start of November. Strained by media harassment and weakened by intermittent drug use, Yoko Ono was admitted to a London hospital on 4 November suffering complications in the middle stages of her pregnancy. She miscarried John Ono Lennon II two weeks later. Thereafter, John and Yoko drifted into a lengthy period of heroin abuse, which effectively eradicated Lennon's influence at a crucial stage of the Beatles' career. "It was not too much fun," he commented later. "I never injected it or anything. We sniffed a little when we were in real pain. People were giving us such a hard time."

Over the next few weeks, Lennon composed a set of song fragments that required little explanation: "Everybody Had a Hard Year," "A Case of the Blues," and the utterly harrowing "Oh My Love," directed toward their dead son. "You had a very strong heartbeat," Lennon wrote, "but that's gone now. Probably we'll forget about you." But only by snorting a little more heroin.

While the situation within Lennon's London flat grew ever more grim, McCartney was flourishing under the heady stimulation of love. At the top of his agenda was the Beatles' return to live performance. As Yoko Ono was being hospitalized, Apple confirmed that the Roundhouse had been booked for ten days before Christmas, so that the group could play three live concerts at the venue. All proceeds would go to charity, and the shows would be filmed by director Michael Lindsay-Hogg for a TV spectacular. "These concerts will be a mind-bender!" proclaimed Apple's Jeremy Banks to the *New Musical Express*. "The Beatles' new album is the incredible achievement of five months' work—and they naturally plan to centre their appearances around these 30 tracks."

The Beatles was released on 22 November, by which time it was clear that both McCartney and Apple had spoken too soon. Far from being signed and sealed, negotiations with the Roundhouse had broken down. Instead, there was talk that the concerts would be staged outside London, maybe even in the Beatles' hometown of Liverpool. But the rapid approach of Christmas, when most venues were already fully booked, meant that the promised concerts would have to be postponed until January.

The other Beatles had virtually abdicated their responsibility for the project, leaving McCartney in complete control. Lennon and Ono were battling narcotic demons at home; Harrison had glimpsed the chimera of artistic freedom in Woodstock, New York, where he spent Thanksgiving with Bob Dylan and members of the Band; and Starr was promoting *Candy,* the movie in which he made his solo debut as an actor.

McCartney remained the media's inside link to the Beatles' future plans. In early December, he was pledging that the promised live shows would still take place: "it will definitely be free, and we may now do it in a TV studio." But his own commitments to producing Mary Hopkin's debut LP for Apple meant that no immediate schedule could be reached.

Still the scenery kept shifting. McCartney settled on a new date for the concert—18 January 1969—and revealed that the Beatles would be performing a mixture of *White Album* songs and new material. But he was unable to obtain a firm commitment to play in front of an audience from the other Beatles. Reluctantly, McCartney had to sacrifice one vital component in his grand scheme.

Eventually, the tangle of messages back and forth across the Atlantic produced a modicum of agreement. The live show would take place somewhere in the world on 18 January, as announced, but in front of a camera crew, not a select bunch of Beatles fans. "All the songs will be new and fresh," announced Apple press officer Derek Taylor. "There'll be no hangover numbers from a year ago, or anything like that." To supervise the filming of the concert, they enlisted Michael Lindsay-Hogg, who had just directed a concert movie for the Rolling Stones—*Rock 'n' Roll Circus.* Lennon and Ono had made a cameo appearance in that film, which may have helped persuade the Beatles that they too should be immortalizing their music-making on celluloid. Besides capturing the concert, Lindsay-Hogg's crew was also hired to film the group's rehearsals for an accompanying documentary. A live album was immediately scheduled for release by March 1969 at the latest.

This was the basis on which Lennon, McCartney, Harrison, and Starr convened at Twickenham Film Studios in southwest London at 10:00 on the morning of 2 January 1969. Ahead lay four weeks of internecine strife

and artistic ennui, which, far from rekindling the Beatles' collective sense of purpose as McCartney had hoped, sealed their collective fate. Through it all, cameras and tape decks were rolling.

"It was time for another Beatles movie," Lennon sneered in a *Rolling Stone* interview at the end of 1970. "Paul wanted us to go on the road or do something. And George and I were going 'mumble . . . we don't want to do the fucker.' He sort of set it up, and there was discussions about where to go and all of that, and I would just tag along, and I had Yoko by then and I was stoned all the time. I just didn't give a shit, you know, nobody did."

Lennon's pointedly one-sided view of the doomed enterprise that became *Let It Be* was at least honest in one respect: his own lack of enthusiasm for the entire exercise. Even at their most positive, the Beatles had always preferred to record in the evening and at night, blinking their

McCartney attempts to rally the troops around the soundboard. Left to right: Ringo, Paul, George, Yoko, John.
Courtesy of Photofest

way home through the emerging dawn light while "straight" people were dragging themselves from their beds.

In January 1969, the Beatles were shown a taste of reality, in the form of early-morning calls and nine-to-five schedules. Lennon, for one, found it oppressive: "We couldn't get into it. It was just a dreadful, dreadful feeling in Twickenham Studio, being filmed all the time. I just wanted them [the film crew] to go away. You couldn't make music at eight in the morning or ten or whatever it was, in a strange place with people filming you and colored lights."

After meeting his first deadline on 2 January, Lennon rarely crawled through the door at Twickenham before midday. By then, the pattern for each session had already been set. McCartney would be there on schedule, vamping through his work in progress for the film crew and building up a rapport with director Lindsay-Hogg. The ever cooperative Starr would be the next to arrive, with tales of the previous night's boozing or TV. Then, without apologies, Lennon and Harrison would make a discreet entrance, and after a round or two of semifriendly badinage, the Beatles would settle down to work—or the avoiding thereof.

The cavernous interior of the Twickenham studio that the Beatles had commandeered was hardly conducive to nurturing the spark of creativity. The group was used to recording in EMI's No. 2 studio on northwest London's Abbey Road, where carefully located screens and baffles obscured the size of the room and lent the surroundings a sense of security. At Twickenham, the Beatles were crammed into one end of a hall with all the intimacy of an aircraft hangar. They were only too aware of the vast open space around them, dotted with cameramen, lighting crew, and their own aides, slumped across the room waiting for instructions. Early in the sessions, McCartney attempted to convince the others that the starkness of their surroundings was a virtue and could be exploited visually: "These songs are our paintings. Get very bright lights so you can see everything, instead of moody lighting. With everything here, it hardly needs scenery. The scenery would just be the other things around, like the scaffolding, the other cameras. I don't dig underestimating what's here." Within days, though, he too had succumbed to the deadening emptiness of Twickenham's distant ceilings and walls.

To counteract the sterility of their environment, the group nestled together around Starr's drum kit, though the eye line between Lennon and McCartney was often broken by the silent presence of Yoko Ono, who sat expressionless at John's side. "[The critics] wrote about her looking miserable in the movie," Lennon complained to *Rolling Stone*'s Jann Wenner at the end of 1970. "You sit through sixty sessions with the most big-headed, uptight people on earth and see what it's fucking like."

Yoko's presence was far from being the only grit jamming up the works. George Harrison had flown back from the United States, where he'd been treated by his peers as a significant musical force, to the creative straitjacket of his junior role in the Beatles. "I spent a long time in the States," he explained in *Crawdaddy* a decade later, "and I had such a good time working with all these different musicians. Then I hung out at Woodstock for Thanksgiving. I felt really good at that time. Then I got back to England for Christmas, and on January 1st [*sic*] we were [due] to start on the thing which turned into *Let It Be.*

"Straightaway it was such weird vibes. I'd been starting to be able to enjoy being a musician, but the moment I got back with the Beatles, it was just too difficult. There were just too many limitations based on our being together for so long. Everybody was sort of pigeonholed. It was frustrating.

"The problem for me was that John and Paul had been writing the songs for so long. It was difficult. They had such a lot of tunes, and they automatically thought that theirs should be the priority, so I'd always have to wait through ten of their songs before they'd even listen to one of mine. It was silly. It was very selfish, actually."

When the Beatles' internal feud reached the law courts, McCartney noted in an affidavit that Harrison had quarreled with the rest of the group from the outset of the *Let It Be* sessions. But George aimed the blame in the opposite direction: "The very first day, Paul went into this 'You do this, you do that, don't do this, don't do that.' I just thought, 'Christ, I thought he'd [have] woken up by now.'"

In McCartney's defense, he was hardly the only member of the Beatles, or their immediate circle, to feel some sense of superiority over the group's youngest member. "One time at the Apple office," Lennon recalled to Peter McCabe and Robert Schonfeld, "I said something to George and he said, 'I'm as intelligent as you, you know.' This must have been resentment, but he could have left any time if I was giving him a hard time. Of course, he's got an inferiority complex from working with Paul and me."

Beatles producer George Martin confirmed to *Melody Maker* in 1971 that Harrison's songwriting had never been taken very seriously: "He'd been awfully poor up to then. Some of the stuff he'd written was very boring. The impression is sometimes given that we put him down. I don't think we ever did that, but possibly we didn't encourage him enough. He'd write, but we wouldn't say, 'What've you got then, George?' We'd say, 'Oh, you've got some more, have you?' I must say that looking back, it was a bit hard on him. It was always slightly condescending. But it was natural, because the others were so talented."

Although it was the chasm between Harrison and McCartney that was highlighted in the *Let It Be* movie, relations between George and John Lennon were scarcely any easier. Harrison seems to have had more trouble than McCartney in relating to Yoko Ono; there was still the legacy of Lennon's disinterest in Harrison's material during the laborious sessions for *The White Album*. John made belated gestures of solidarity after the group had split up: "I can't speak for George, but I know pretty well that we got fed up being sidemen for Paul." But as the early days at Twickenham became bogged down in boredom, Harrison was as enraged by Lennon's refusal to communicate as he was by McCartney's condescending attitude.

When the cameras began to roll on 2 January 1969, the Beatles had precisely sixteen days to prepare an album's worth of new material for their live concert and TV special. Shortly after 10:00 that morning, John Lennon, Yoko Ono, and George Harrison arrived at Twickenham Studios. While the Beatles' road manager, Mal Evans, set up their equipment, Michael Lindsay-Hogg's crew was already in position. Besides the film cameras scattered around the room, two Nagra tape recorders maintained almost unbroken audio monitoring of the sessions—capturing the Beatles' music and also, crucially, their conversations. Over the next four weeks, these Nagra tapes documented the everyday trivia of the group's working life. More important, they bore witness to an unfolding series of dramas, conflicts, and power plays. It was the Beatles' misfortune that the most self-destructive month of their career was recorded for posterity in damning detail.

At that first session, there was no hint of the crises to come. The tapes began to roll as Lennon and Harrison swapped fragments of their new songs. Lennon offered "Don't Let Me Down" and "Dig a Pony"; Harrison responded with "All Things Must Pass" and "Let It Down." Amicably, they settled on "Don't Let Me Down" for their initial rehearsal.

By the time Starr and McCartney reached the studio, Lennon and Harrison had already worked up some rough harmonies for the song. Running it through for the others, John regularly segued into a showy piece of guitar picking, obviously much practiced, over which he sang vaguely, "Here is the sun king." Over the next four weeks, such improvisations would be extracted and molded into songs—or, just as often, toyed with, then forgotten forever.

Almost immediately, the Beatles were unsettled by the size of the film studio and its spartan facilities. "Where's the console and all that?" Harrison asked plaintively as the session began. "Where are the mixer and the eight-tracks?" "We'd do better to rehearse in a small room," Lennon added.

Another concern was the lack of up-tempo material the four Beatles had brought to the sessions. "We'll probably write some fast ones here, all of us," Lennon muttered hopefully, as he vamped at a riff from his 1968 composition "Revolution." In answer, Harrison sang a line or two from Bob Dylan's "I Shall Be Released"—an escape route that he continued to use throughout the sessions.

It wasn't just the apposite nature of Dylan's lyrics, or memories of his recent stay with the songwriter in Woodstock, that prompted George to drift into Dylan's songs whenever the tension at Twickenham mounted. Like virtually everyone who'd heard them, Harrison had been struck by the intimacy and enigmatic humor of the home demos—the so-called *Basement Tapes*—that Dylan and the Band had taped in the summer of 1967. Not intended for public release, the recordings had nonetheless circulated among the rock aristocracy, and Harrison had brought back copies from the United States for the Beatles. He must have hoped that his group might be able to conjure up a little *Basement Tapes* spirit during these Twickenham sessions.

The nature of their film project ensured that George's optimism would be disappointed. Indeed, the presence of Lindsay-Hogg and his crew dampened the Beatles' enthusiasm from the start. "Are you record-

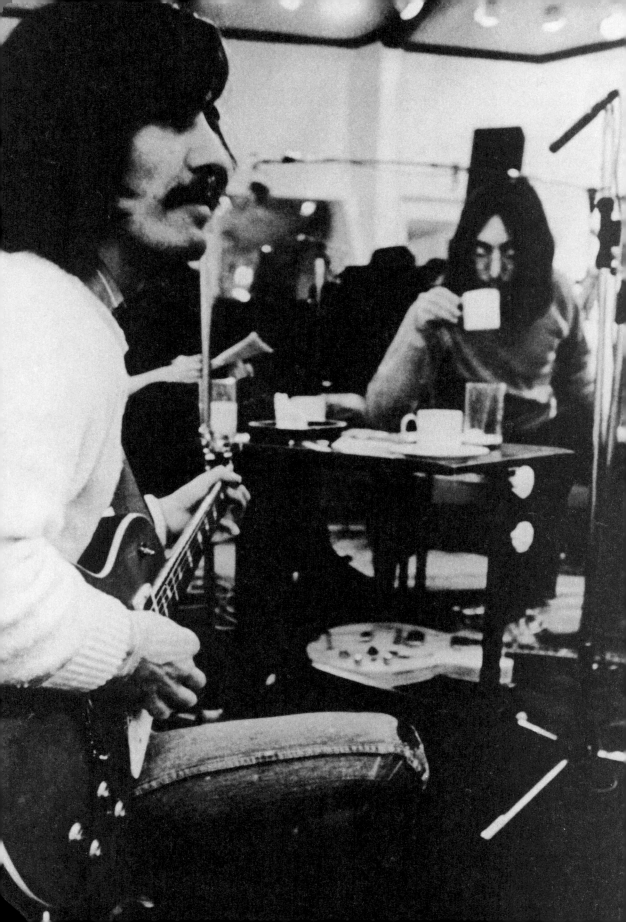

ing our conversations?" Harrison asked in disbelief, as the director rearranged the microphones. "We should rehearse in a room, or in a corner, or something," Lennon repeated. "Maybe we should learn a few songs," was Harrison's sardonic response. But he admitted that "I don't think this is a very good acoustic place."

Across the studio, Beatles record producer George Martin—present out of courtesy rather than duty, because the group wasn't officially recording at this point—was making the entirely opposite point, praising the sound that engineer Glyn Johns had achieved. Johns, a veteran of sessions with the Stones, the Who, and the Kinks, among others, was a novice with the Beatles, but confident enough of his role to intervene when the discussion turned to possible venues for the live show. He suggested Arabia, and Lindsay-Hogg's filmic imagination was seized by visions of two thousand Arabs watching by torchlight.

But the Beatles had already discussed the subject, and one member had reached a definite decision. "I think you'll find we're not going abroad," McCartney told Lindsay-Hogg firmly. "Ringo's said he doesn't want to go." Then, remembering how the group had toured Australia in 1964 with a substitute drummer when Starr had been ill, he added, "But us and Jimmy Nicol might go instead . . ."

Throughout the conversation, Lindsay-Hogg kept plugging away at the idea of going overseas, to McCartney's initial amusement, but eventually Paul tired of the director's continual prodding. Lindsay-Hogg did convince him of one thing: the benefits of playing outdoors. The problem now was to find a location within Britain that wouldn't be ruined by the vagaries of a British winter.

Another dilemma was posed by Lennon, who had arrived at the session with a song that was a collection of fragments rather than one structured whole. Gently, McCartney pulled "Don't Let Me Down" into shape, suggesting that they augment the group with a keyboard player. He proposed Nicky Hopkins, who'd played on "Revolution"; Harrison reckoned that Paul could play the piano, and that they should find someone who could play stand-up bass. Feeling his natural role in the group was under threat, McCartney squashed that idea, and the session drifted on.

Besides "Don't Let Me Down," McCartney led the group through "I've Got a Feeling," which incorporated Lennon's "Everybody Had a Hard Year" as a countermelody, in an arrangement that had obviously been dis-

George works on a song while John attempts to revive himself with a cup of coffee.

cussed the previous year. He also introduced a brand-new song, "Two of Us," and the first day's session ended with a lengthy teaching session as McCartney honed the structure, while gently persuading Lennon to play the correct chords. With three songs rehearsed to some level of competence, the Twickenham sessions had begun satisfactorily enough.

John was the last to arrive on the morning of 3 January, missing the unveiling of McCartney's latest song in progress, "Let It Be." Paul and George then encouraged Ringo to play his new material. Starr vamped his way apologetically through a few lines apiece of "Taking a Trip to Carolina" and "Picasso"—simplistic, country-flavored tunes that, as he confessed wryly, "are exactly the same!"

There was little hint of tension between McCartney and Harrison as the subject turned to George's material. George confessed that he'd considered the possibility of playing his songs solo at the live show; rather than shouting this idea down, McCartney encouraged it, only for Harrison to change his mind. As he began to demonstrate "All Things Must Pass," McCartney and Starr played along tentatively, as if a solid arrangement might be instantly within reach.

The bonhomie survived Lennon's eventual arrival, upon which the band drifted into what became a familiar routine throughout these sessions: a disorganized, but joyous, medley of rock 'n' roll favorites. In keeping with the idea that the live show should feature songs old and new, McCartney led the band into Lennon's "I'm So Tired"; John reciprocated with a good-humored pastiche of Paul's "Ob-La-Di, Ob-La-Da." McCartney improvised a rocker about "a hole-in-the-heart case," but eventually the group remembered why they were there and started work on "Don't Let Me Down."

For light relief, they exhumed "The One after 909," one of the earliest Lennon/McCartney originals, which dated back to the late '50s. "I always meant to change the words," Lennon said sheepishly. Because they'd performed and even recorded the song earlier in the decade, it fell quickly into place. Soon, a question about working methods arose: "Maybe we should just do it without practicing," Harrison suggested. "Practicing will fuck it up." McCartney disagreed, but offered a compromise: "We'll just know where we're going. We won't arrange it." The question at the heart of the discussion—should they perfect each song in turn, concentrating on details from the start, or merely assemble a collection of rough arrangements?—would come to haunt the Twickenham sessions.

The revival of "The One after 909" prompted Lennon and McCartney to rack their brains for other vintage Beatles originals—country-flavored tunes like "Because You Know I Love You So" and "Won't You Please Say Goodbye"—otherwise undocumented in the group's recording career. Memories of the '50s helped them drift into a rock 'n' roll jam session: they'd now been playing for more than an hour, most of it devoted to avoiding the repertoire for their live show. Eventually they picked up "Two of Us" from the previous night, but McCartney was quickly dispirited by the lack of progress. "We'll never get that," he complained, before suggesting they break for lunch.

The creative impasse was still firmly in place that afternoon. "Shall we learn another one?" asked McCartney encouragingly. Harrison immediately led them into a vintage rocker, "Short Fat Fannie." With that finished, McCartney tried again: "What number shall we do next?" Lennon responded with another oldie, "Midnight Special."

Since the previous day, the group had been furnished with lyric and chord sheets for the songs they'd agreed to rehearse, and Lennon unenthusiastically recited the titles: "'All Things Must Pass,' 'She Came in through the Bathroom Window,' 'Maxwell's Silver Hammer' . . . I've got one verse of one," he offered instead, and began to play "Gimme Some Truth," for which McCartney immediately suggested a middle eight. The addition was duly incorporated into the song, and retained (uncredited) when Lennon eventually recorded it for his *Imagine* LP in 1971.

Quiet persistence finally paid off for Harrison, who was allowed to lead the band through "All Things Must Pass." He explained how he'd been inspired by a psychedelic prayer written by LSD guru Timothy Leary, and that he already knew how he wanted the song to sound. "We're pretending to be the Band on this one," he said. "I have been on all of them," Lennon quipped. But little of the Band's camaraderie surfaced over the next thirty minutes, as McCartney strained for a vocal harmony and Lennon stabbed erratically at an organ. "Really, I should play this on acoustic guitar," Harrison offered. "But how am I gonna do that on your famous TV show?" Gamely, he requested backing vocals from Paul, who yawned conspicuously. "Sing, John," McCartney called out, but Lennon ignored him.

An uncharacteristically light moment in the studio. Left to right: George (reading *Disc and Music Echo* magazine), Paul, and John.
Courtesy of Photofest

The session was once again drifting into ennui, and Harrison turned to McCartney. "You're so full of shit, man!" he said slyly. When Paul gave a surprised grunt, George explained that he was merely quoting from a Michael McClure play he'd just seen, but the point had been made.

The discussion turned to safer territory. "Are we going to do any oldies on the show?" Harrison asked. "It would be nice, and it would get over that initial thing of us hitting them with all new stuff." Lennon suggested some radical reinterpretations of their back catalog, in the vein of Joe Cocker's "With a Little Help from My Friends." "I've been doing a lot of 'Help!' recently," he added, while Harrison suggested they try the *Beatles for Sale* song "Every Little Thing." Unhelpfully, Michael Lindsay-Hogg chimed in with a list of his favorite Little Richard oldies.

Slowly, the conversation drifted into dissension. Lennon opined that it was a stupid idea to work up a set of new songs one month, then have to go straight into recording yet more fresh material immediately afterward. McCartney saw his cue: "We should organise our career. That's the idea of this, to get it so we enjoy doing this again. Would you like to do a live show, lads?"

Harrison adopted the unresponsive attitude that became his motif throughout the sessions: "It's like hard work to do it. I don't want to work, really. It's a drag to get your guitar at eight in the morning, when you're not ready for it." Then, aware that he might have offended McCartney, he backtracked: "There's so much material for us to get out, and there's no one better to get it out with than us, for me, really. Heart of hearts." After that, he had no defense when Paul set about teaching the group his mock nursery rhyme, "Maxwell's Silver Hammer," ending the second session on a less-than-productive note.

Two days' respite over the weekend robbed the Twickenham sessions of any slight momentum that might have been built up. On 6 January, the Beatles seemed reluctant to begin work, arriving with a trail of excuses—hangovers, insomnia—that had dampened their enthusiasm. As he watched his celebrity subjects ignoring the schedule, which called for the live show to take place in just two weeks, movie director Michael Lindsay-Hogg grew concerned. "We ought to think about the show," he nagged McCartney. Paul sneered back: "We *are* thinking about the show." The discussion turned a few more circles. McCartney agreed with Lindsay-Hogg's suggestion that they should play in front of a sizable audience, whatever venue they chose. Harrison chipped in: "I think we should forget the whole idea of the show." "I'll go along with that," muttered McCartney in a rare moment of cynicism.

Not that Harrison had much cause for enthusiasm that Monday morning. His insomnia aside, he'd arrived at the session bearing the news that he'd written a gospel song. "According to Saint who?" Lennon snapped back. "According to the Lord," George said piously. After a brief attempt to interest the group in his song, he set "Hear Me Lord" aside for his own solo project.

So the Beatles drifted uneasily into their predictable diet of oldies, forgetting their doubts and differences for a few minutes amid vintage Carl

Perkins and Larry Williams songs. But the vexed subject of the live concert continued to loom over the sessions. For twenty minutes, McCartney, Harrison, Lindsay-Hogg, and Yoko Ono tossed around ideas, while Lennon and Starr remained resolutely silent. The eerie void left by Lennon's refusal to participate soured the atmosphere. In his place, Ono contributed a stream of bizarre, conceptual, and often insensitive suggestions, seemingly unaware that the group's future was actually the oblique subject under discussion.

Distanced from their audience since they'd abandoned touring in 1966, the Beatles viewed the prospect of renewed contact with suspicion. "It would be just our luck to get a load of cunts in there," Harrison muttered as McCartney and George Martin tried to remind him that the group might be stimulated by the presence of a sympathetic crowd. Ono came up with the intriguing but ill-timed idea that the group should play to twenty thousand empty seats—"the invisible nameless everybody in the world"—or that they should select an audience, restricting it to their families or even to royalty. McCartney did his best to be conciliatory, offering the solution that since "we are doing two shows, we could do one night to silence, and one to those seats filled." "But part of the documentary is you playing to silence," Lindsay-Hogg intervened, aware that at this moment the Beatles weren't even playing. He preferred a seaside location and was about to wax lyrical about the torchlit Arabs again when McCartney cut him short: "We've decided we're not going abroad."

It was Harrison who came up with the most constructive suggestion. Borrowing Derek Taylor's axiom that one should "create and preserve the image of one's choice," he pointed out that "we can create another image. We could be a nightclub act, or anything." McCartney, who'd been suggesting for months that the Beatles go back to the club circuit under a pseudonym, enthusiastically agreed. Movie producer Denis O'Dell changed tack, envisaging the Beatles performing to an audience of Old Masters in an art gallery. Not surprisingly, Yoko Ono caught the symbolic strength of this idea and told Lindsay-Hogg that he should also be filming the Beatles in their homes, from dawn to dusk. Sadly, Harrison's response to the idea of a camera crew waking him at dawn isn't recorded.

Having maintained an undignified silence throughout this discussion, as if Yoko were speaking for him, Lennon roused himself enough to begin work on "Don't Let Me Down." Slowly, the atmosphere deteriorated.

Harrison moaned that if they weren't careful, the song "could sound like the same old shit." "Well, I *like* the same old shit," Lennon countered. A couple of abortive run-throughs later, Harrison cast his verdict on the entire session: "It's awful."

Dropping "Don't Let Me Down," they switched to "Two of Us," which had been rehearsed at some length four days earlier. Not that Lennon remembered: "Am I singing on this, or not?" Once he'd been persuaded that he was, the Beatles stumbled through attempt after attempt, continually caught up by minor details. "Let's get it, so we know it, simply," said McCartney pleadingly, "then we can add to it. We don't know any one song yet, straight. We keep trying to get the bits right."

His efforts were in vain, and he and Harrison slipped into the argument that can be glimpsed briefly in the *Let It Be* movie, although it is transplanted, to give the impression that they had fallen out over the guitar break in another song, "I've Got a Feeling." As the original film footage reveals, it wasn't individual notes that sparked the confrontation, but the much broader issue of attitude and commitment.

Throughout it all, McCartney is cast as the reluctant, indeed embarrassed, cheerleader. "What I want to say is, come on and play, but I can't, so we get into that one," he complained, trying to hint (but not actually say) that he was tired of being responsible for directing every session. Harrison replied with an exasperating, teenage insolence, masked as cooperation: "I'll just play the chords if you like." Forced to explain what he wanted George to infer, Paul was set back on the defensive: "You're always trying to make it sound as if I'm saying that," he said patiently— "that" being an explicit criticism of Harrison's musicianship. "But I'm only trying to help you, and I always hear myself trying to annoy you." "You're not annoying me," Harrison rejoined coldly, "you don't annoy me anymore." The rift had gone deeper than that.

Harrison's brattish intransigence pushed McCartney onward, into a disagreement he was anxious to avoid, especially in public; "I can't do it on film," he said, in a bid for George's sympathy. Harrison remained silent, so McCartney made a bid for the moral high ground: "We've only got twelve more days, so we've got to do this methodically. I just hear myself being the only one [of us] saying it. I never get any support." Nor did he now. He stumbled into deeper waters: "I'm not trying to get you, I'm just trying to say, 'Look, lads, the band. Let's do it like this.'" At this,

George's patience snapped: "I'll play what you want me to play. I won't play at all if you don't want me to. Whatever it is that will please you, I'll do it." His grim face suggested otherwise.

McCartney regrouped: "Look, it's gotta sound as if it's improved [since last week]." Harrison was dismissive: "It sounds to me as if it's a waste of time, [right] from when we started it today." Exhausted by his lack of progress, Paul turned to John for support, or a share of the blame, or anything to break the tension between him and Harrison. "We waste a hell of a lot of time," McCartney began; Lennon said nothing. "That's what I'm scared of," Paul continued, "me [always] being the boss. I have been for a couple of years." It was a statement of absolute truth, which drew no response from the other Beatles. Sensing at least a hint of victory, McCartney laid down a ground rule: "We should all arrange our own tunes, and if we want any improvisation, we should say." This was passed without a murmur, and the music-making eventually resumed.

Harrison soon felt sufficiently relaxed to ask McCartney for instructions. "Do you want it more countrified?" he asked as they returned to "Two of Us." But Paul couldn't forget what had just happened. "I don't mind, I'll go where it goes," he muttered, before blurting out the truth: "I can't talk . . . I daren't put my foot anywhere."

After that, it was a tribute to the Beatles' collective memory that they achieved substantial progress that afternoon on Harrison's "All Things Must Pass," and then slipped easily into McCartney's "She Came in through the Bathroom Window." All too symbolically, McCartney exited the session busking a line from a new song: "Boy, you gotta carry that weight."

The four Beatles gathered for a business meeting that night to discuss progress on various Apple projects and to come a little closer to a decision on their live show. By the following morning, 7 January, much of the previous afternoon's angst had dissipated. McCartney arrived early, showing off his new material to Lindsay-Hogg and the crew: "The Long and Winding Road" and a medley of "Golden Slumbers" and "Carry That Weight." While he vamped through a series of piano improvisations, Harrison and Starr chatted on the other side of the room, unaware that they were being taped. George explained how he'd found a picture of the Beatles at the maharishi's meditation center in Rishikesh the previous spring, and how it was apparent that several of their party—notably

Controlled (?) chaos.
George, Paul, John.
COURTESY OF PHOTOFEST

McCartney, his then girlfriend Jane Asher, and Lennon's first wife, Cynthia Lennon—were completely out of sync with what was going on. Like kids talking behind teacher's back, the two Beatles sniggered at Paul's lack of understanding.

Their backroom humor seemed briefly to clear the mood for the rehearsals. McCartney improvised a bass guitar line, beginning to spout out a rough blueprint for what would become "Get Back." Harrison tried to interest the others in another new song, "For You Blue," only to find that they talked while he played. Another suggestion came to mind: "Shall we do some other people's tunes as well on the show?" "I don't know any," said Lennon, in a tone masquerading as humor. "I can only just bear doing your lot's tunes, let alone strangers'."

But instead of drifting into anyone's tunes, the Beatles turned once again to the vexed subject of why they were there, whether they were ever going to play a live show, and what the movie was for. "It's not as good as it could be yet," McCartney said of the plan for the film. "We haven't thought of a great idea yet." "What do we do if we can't think of a gimmick?" asked Lennon, before supplying his own answer: "The worst we'll have is a documentary of us making an LP." It was the first time that any of the group had glimpsed into the future and realized what the *Let It Be* movie would become.

"We've been very negative since Mr. Epstein passed away," said McCartney philosophically. While Lennon countered with a plaintive platitude, "The incentive is to communicate"—as if he'd been doing anything of the sort since the sessions began—McCartney pressed home his point: "There is no one there to say 'Do it.' Your daddy goes away at a certain point of your life. It's discipline we lack." His parental rebuke gradually rekindled the tension of the previous day. As Paul mentioned Apple artist Jackie Lomax as an example of someone with a perfect attitude in the studio—"From beginning to end, he was like, 'Gotta do it'"—Harrison countered dryly: "Work with him, then." "Well, you used to do it, lads," McCartney cracked with false humor. As usual, Harrison took refuge in a Bob Dylan lyric: "I was so much older then, I'm younger than that now."

Unable to watch another day's rehearsal dissolve into navel-gazing, Michael Lindsay-Hogg intervened: "Do you want to perform to an audience, or do you just see yourself as a recording group?" It was, after all, rather crucial to his project. McCartney managed a conciliatory air: "I think there's something in the performing thing."

But Harrison was less positive about contributing anything of himself to the show, or the project as a whole. "I don't want to do any of my songs on the show," he announced blithely, "because they'll turn out shitty, they'll come out like a compromise." And compromise was no longer an option. McCartney attempted to reason with him: "Look, last year you were telling me, 'You can do anything you want' . . . I think we're very good. We can get it together if we think we want to do these songs great." Already, by 7 January, that had become a very moot point.

Lindsay-Hogg brought them back to the movie, and the location for the live show. Why wouldn't they go abroad? "We're not going away," McCartney repeated for at least the third time. "That's a group decision." The conceptualists took over again, as the director suggested playing to a bunch of sick kids in a hospital and Harrison declared that the show should have a political, or at least social, message. McCartney relished the idea of trespassing, being carted away by the police in midnumber; Lindsay-Hogg could visualize the tears in children's eyes if they played an orphanage.

Throughout this discussion, Lennon said nothing, picking away at his guitar as if to distance himself from the conversation. Possibly his alienation was drug induced; more likely, he was simply out of sync with the group and their aims. "What do you think?" McCartney asked him pointedly. "About what?" Lennon replied. Paul didn't try to involve him again.

"Hear no evil, speak no evil, see no evil," quipped Harrison, pointing in turn to McCartney, Lennon, and Starr. Roused for once to speech, Ringo echoed Lennon: "I'm not interested."

Faced with complete withdrawal by two of the group and outright cynicism from the third, McCartney finally lost his temper: "I don't see why any of you, if you're not interested, get yourselves into this. What's it for? It can't be for the money. Why are you here? I'm here because I want to do a show, but I really don't feel an awful lot of support." He paused for a response, but the other Beatles said nothing. It was the most telling moment of the entire Twickenham sessions.

John and Yoko.

A few minutes later, McCartney tried again, pleading directly to Lennon for sympathy: "I feel terrible. Imagine if you were the only one interested. You don't say anything." Lennon managed a one-line reply: "I've said what I've been thinking"—exactly nothing.

Thrown by this blatant display of apathy, McCartney soldiered on alone, as if logic could conquer disinterest. He reminded the group that at the previous night's meeting, it had been their ultraloyal yes-man of a road manager, Mal Evans, who had confronted them with the fact that they needed to make a decision about the live show—today. If even Mal was speaking out, McCartney concluded, then they must be in trouble. "There's only two choices: we're gonna do it or we're not gonna do it. And I want a decision," he insisted. "Because I'm not interested in spending my fucking days farting around here, while everyone makes up their mind whether they want to do it or not. I'll do it. If everyone else wants to do it, great. But I don't have to be here."

None of the other Beatles said a word. Unwilling to admit total defeat, McCartney reminded them that they'd been through the same situation the previous year, while they were making *The White Album:* "The album was worse than this. Remember, the whole idea: did we want to do it? We all phoned Neil [Aspinall, Apple's managing director] individually, saying: 'Can you get 'em together?' Instead of asking each other, we went to Neil. We should just have [had] it out."

Which is exactly what McCartney wanted to do: "If this one turns out like that, it should definitely be the last—for all of us. There's no point hanging on." Bluff or bravado, McCartney's gesture, putting the Beatles' future on the line, at least drew a response from Harrison: "That's it." But George didn't come up with the positive arguments Paul wanted to hear. Instead, he reminded the bassist that "the Beatles have been in the doldrums for at least a year."

Aware that his tactic of threatening the unthinkable had failed—Harrison was only too willing to embrace the unthinkable—McCartney went back on himself: "When we do get together, we just talk about the fucking past. We're like OAPs [old-age pensioners], saying, 'Do you remember the days when we used to rock?' Well, we're here now, we can still do it." Harrison turned away to talk to Michael Lindsay-Hogg, Lennon and Starr kept their mouths firmly closed, and McCartney finally abandoned hope of applying the balm of logic to the Beatles' wounds.

Now Harrison went on the offensive. He'd heard McCartney's side; Paul would have to hear his. He encapsulated his discontent in a single sentence: "I've got about twenty songs, but I know very well that the moment I bring them into the studio, it's like this," and he blew a convincing raspberry to illustrate Lennon and McCartney's degree of interest in his work.

Harrison was ready to take McCartney's position to its logical conclusion: "Maybe we should get a divorce." Paul wasn't prepared to let him take all the credit: "Well, I said that at the last meeting. It's getting near it." Divorce being a subject close to his heart, as he was waiting for Yoko Ono's separation from Tony Cox to be confirmed legally, John Lennon finally intervened: "Who'd get the children?" "Dick James," quipped McCartney, fingering the Beatles' music publisher, and for a few seconds the group was united in sarcastic laughter.

Sensing a brief rapport with the others, McCartney gently steered the conversation back to business: "It is so silly for us to crack up. There's no point. The only possible direction is the other way." He turned to John and reminded him that he and Yoko had been performing live in recent weeks, if only in a white bag on the stage of the Royal Albert Hall during an underground art experience. Lennon had obviously used that as a bargaining device in the discussions about the movie, to prove that he could appear in public without the other Beatles. McCartney continued: "It's silly for you to come in and talk down to us about it." Then he decided to force the point home. "Well, actually, your way out is not to talk rather than talk down to us. Remember, I think I'm talking down to you."

This confused, crippling conversation was somehow the signal for the Beatles to begin work. As if the anguished discussion about the entire future of the group hadn't taken place, Lennon, McCartney, Harrison, and Starr returned to their instruments and prepared to resume the rehearsal. McCartney called out for "I've Got a Feeling," and Lennon plunged into the first verse of "She Came in through the Bathroom Window," getting through several lines to the accompaniment of hysterical laughter from his colleagues before he realized his mistake. That dissolved the tension, and the remainder of the session was devoted to music—ragged, confused, unfocused—but music nonetheless.

McCartney's "Oh! Darling" and "Maxwell's Silver Hammer" dominated the early stages, before Lennon announced that he wanted a second shot at "Across the Universe," having been unhappy with the recording the Beatles had made eleven months earlier. This rehearsal was doomed by the fact that Lennon was unable to remember the lyrics: after singing the chorus line, "Nothing's gonna change my world," John cried out, "I wish it fucking would!" to which McCartney replied mock-scoldingly: "You must take control, John!" After a brief jam on some old rockers, "Across the Universe" sounded even less appetizing, so the menu reverted to the songs they already knew, like "The One after 909" and "Don't Let Me Down." Even if little progress had been made, mere survival was, under the circumstances, an achievement in itself.

George Harrison arrived at Twickenham on the morning of 8 January with a new song that encapsulated what he'd heard from the other Beatles: "I Me Mine." "I don't care if you don't want it on your show," he announced to no one in particular. "I don't give a fuck. It'll go in the musical"—a project about life at Apple that he was proposing to write with Derek Taylor. McCartney, though, was receptive to George's new tune, each going out of his way to mend the previous day's wounds. McCartney even offered the guitarist a pair of boots he'd never worn.

Recognizing the danger of talk, the Beatles settled immediately into a unifying jam session. They were at their most eclectic, one minute romping through '50s rockers like "Honey Hush," the next twisting the words to the Hare Krishna mantra or reviving yet more golden oldies from the prefame Lennon/McCartney songbook.

Harrison's "All Things Must Pass" was their next target, as Lennon and McCartney briefly locked into the spirit of the Band with some harmony vocals. But when George introduced "I Me Mine" to Lennon, the reaction was hardly complimentary. "We'll use it for a commercial," John snapped. "It's fine," he then conceded dryly, "but what do we do about it? It's very short. And it sounds hard to do." Having invented at least two reasons for ignoring the song, he then proceeded to satirize it, McCartney indulgently joining in.

After a while, Paul donned the mantle of leadership one more time, facetiously asking Lennon, "Haven't you written anything?" "No," said Lennon bluntly. "We're going to be facing a crisis," Paul added, eliciting a sarcastic reply: "When I'm up against the wall, Paul, you'll find that I'm at my best." Able to say in jest what he really thought, McCartney nagged: "I wish you'd come up with the goods." "I think I've got Sunday off," Lennon said laconically. Paul adopted a parental tone: "I hope you can deliver." "I'm hoping for a little rock 'n' roller," was Lennon's retort.

Ironically, it was McCartney who added some rock 'n' roll to the session, inventing a middle section for "I Me Mine," then driving Harrison and Starr through it while Lennon and Ono waltzed erratically around the studio floor. It was a stunning demonstration of the Beatles' powers when they were all focused on the same object. "I Me Mine" had been written and virtually perfected in less than a day. But there was no payback for this effort: it was never performed again during the sessions.

In the absence of Lennon tunes, McCartney began to guide the group through the skeletal forms of "Let It Be" and "The Long and Winding Road." Harrison offered functional accompaniment; Lennon paid little attention at all.

The day ended with a bizarre discussion about—what else?—the location of the live show. Once again, Michael Lindsay-Hogg and film producer Denis O'Dell were pushing for an overseas setting, and for the first time, the Beatles didn't immediately quash the idea. "We could give away tickets here," said McCartney, "and the ticket would include a boat journey as well." Lindsay-Hogg had dreamed up the ridiculous idea of allotting the Beatles individual code names, prompting this immortal exchange with John Lennon: "We've got to get the right audience for Russia." "Oh Russia! That'd be great!" "No, that's Ringo's code name."

It was left to Harrison to inject some realism into the debate: "What's the point of going abroad, apart from getting a quick holiday? I'd much rather do the show and then go on holiday." Once again, Lindsay-Hogg led the small talk down avenues of confusion. "How about France coming in?" he asked. "I can't go to France," said Harrison in an alarmed tone, aware that within the month he would be tried, in his absence, on a minor assault charge resulting from a fracas with a journalist in 1968. "No," the director had to explain again, "that's your code name."

If nothing else, the discussion succeeded in awakening Lennon from his self-induced torpor. Though he was alarmed by the idea of the Beatles shipbound with several thousand fans—or "a load of mental deficients," as he put it concisely—he was entranced by the theatricality of an outdoor setting, "as the sun comes up, just on the middle eight." While Harrison continually stressed the practicalities—how they would get a boat, who'd ship the equipment, where they could get the amplifiers— Lennon briefly became the group's in-house enthusiast: "We're bound to get something from it, if only a good feeling about singing in the sun, like we did on the roof in India."

Lindsay-Hogg pushed the Beatles for a vote, sensing that he might be on the verge of triumph, but Harrison countered: "I think the idea of a boat is insane, very expensive and insane." McCartney and Lennon ended the discussion right there, Paul singing "cut out the bullshit" under his breath while Lindsay-Hogg was still clamoring for a decision. John delivered a parting shot: "Don't forget, we want a boat full of mental deficients and dwarves, by Friday!"

Thursday, 9 January, dawned with McCartney at the piano, busking on another batch of half-finished songs, including "Her Majesty" and "Another Day." Flushed by his success at persuading two of his colleagues to play "I Me Mine" the previous day, Harrison was making the case for another shot at "For You Blue." But after a few minutes, the Beatles switched to "Two of Us," which had lost its cohesion since the start of the week. When McCartney scolded Lennon for being off mike,

A dismaying playback.
Ringo, George Martin, Paul,
George, Yoko, John, camera-
man.
COURTESY OF PHOTOFEST

John muttered just loud enough for everyone to hear, "Don't bitch about it." After twenty minutes, the song was worked back into some kind of cohesive shape, and the Beatles capitalized on the moment by delivering the best version of "Don't Let Me Down" to date.

After improvising a risqué rocker called "Suzy's Parlour," the group was on a roll. They dragged "I've Got a Feeling" from chaos to competence, then turned the same trick with McCartney's "She Came in through the Bathroom Window," before Paul led them into "Get Back," which had acquired a tentative structure since its debut the previous week. At this point it was a naive piece of social commentary about British immigration policy, but at least it was "the fast one" that Lennon had been demanding all along.

"Across the Universe" halted the momentum, as it slouched toward inertia. "There's an Oriental influence that shouldn't really be there," McCartney noted at one point. Bearing in mind Lennon's subsequent assertion that "Get Back" was aimed at Yoko Ono, that's an intriguingly ambiguous comment.

The session then descended into mayhem. "We're tired, so maybe we should cut out the wine," Harrison suggested as the band slipped into a series of cover versions that veered from satirical ("Move It") to hysterical (Lennon and McCartney's screaming match through "House of the

Rising Sun"). Pleasantly inebriated, John and Paul indulged in some verbal jousting, improvising a silly ditty called "Commonwealth," and then striking up a blues riff over which they competed to offer up the names of friends and enemies—each person greeted with a hearty "Get off!" from Lennon. When that broke down, the impatient Harrison offered his usual sulk: "I do one, but it's acoustic guitar with no backing." "Get off!" shrieked Lennon, and the jam resumed. The day ended with a rather more coherent attempt to learn "Let It Be." Discussion about the live show had, for once, thankfully been avoided.

The morning of 10 January was a more sober reprise of the previous day, as the Beatles perfected the electric arrangement of "Two of Us," then attempted less successfully to tame "Get Back." There was little hint of tension among the musicians, but no suggestion either that they were any closer to bridging their gulf over the live show and the future of the band.

By lunchtime, it seems that Harrison could restrain himself no longer. While McCartney and Starr watched silently, George apparently confronted the band with a litany of complaints. Their exact nature is unknown, but easy to imagine: take your pick from Lennon's refusal to communicate with the other Beatles, his lack of enthusiasm for Harrison's songs, McCartney's insistence on telling George how to play, or the trio's willingness to take Lindsay-Hogg's plans for a boat trip to Africa seriously. Lennon appears to have shrugged off the criticism sarcastically. Back within earshot of the film crew's microphones, Harrison coolly announced: "I'm leaving the group." "When?" asked Lennon. "Now," he replied. Even then, there was no serious discussion. "You can replace me," Harrison offered. "Put an ad in the *New Musical Express* and get a few people in." Then he calmly strolled out of the studio.

The walkout has gone down in history as a dispute between George and Paul, chiefly on the evidence of the mild disagreement over a guitar part documented in the *Let It Be* film. "There's a scene in the movie where Paul and I are having an argument," George explained to *Crawdaddy* a decade later, "and we were trying to cover it up. Then the next scene I'm not there, and Yoko's just screaming, doing her screeching number." In fact, no footage of the other Beatles jamming with Yoko was included in the movie, though that unique collaboration did take place shortly after Harrison's departure.

Ringo Starr's memory of events in a 1971 *Melody Maker* interview was similar: "George had to leave because he thought Paul was dominating him. Well, he was."

"I didn't care if it was the Beatles," Harrison recalled, "I was getting out." He drove home and channeled his bitterness and anger into writing yet another song, "Wah-Wah," to alleviate the crushing headache triggered by the mounting tension. "'Wah-Wah' was a headache as well as a foot pedal," he explained obliquely the following year.

In his absence, the three remaining Beatles continued to rehearse, since there was nothing else to do. Presumably as a comment on Harrison's departure, Lennon began to play an appalling version of the Who's mini–rock opera "A Quick One While He's Away." When he decided it was time for a guitar solo, he called out "Okay, George, take it" to the empty chair. No one laughed.

As John, Paul, and Ringo wasted time pretending everything was normal, Michael Lindsay-Hogg and Apple's Neil Aspinall discussed George's decision. "They're going to have a meeting on Sunday," Aspinall confided. But he expressed his sympathy for "the box George is in"—that is, the way that the others either downplayed or changed his songs. "A few months of that would be enough for me," Aspinall concluded. "But eight years . . ."

Lennon wandered over to show that he, for one, wasn't concerned. "I think that if George doesn't come back by Monday or Tuesday, we'll have to get Eric Clapton to play with us," he declared, having been impressed by his jam session with Clapton at the Rolling Stones' *Rock 'n' Roll Circus* in December. "The point is: if George leaves, do we want to carry on the Beatles? I do. We should just get other members and carry on."

Ringo Starr was more dubious, while Lindsay-Hogg offered a face-saving solution for his film: "For the show, we could just say George was sick." Lennon had no time for that idea: "If he leaves, he leaves," he said dismissively. The director was still concerned about his project: "What's the consensus: do you want to go on with the show?" Lennon, acting as group spokesman now that it was too late, was adamant: "Yeah. If he doesn't come back by Tuesday, we get Clapton." Sadly, further discussion was cut short by a churlish, attention-seeking display from Yoko Ono, who decided to launch into calling and screaming Lennon's name. Amid the noise, Lindsay-Hogg had time to put John's suggestion to Ringo Starr, who was the Beatle most likely to side with Harrison. His reply was blunt and to the point: "Do it."

On Sunday, 12 January, all four Beatles met at Ringo Starr's house to debate the future of their film project. None of them has ever discussed this meeting in public, but its outcome was not entirely unpredictable. McCartney and Starr turned up for work at Twickenham the following morning; Harrison visited his parents instead; Lennon and Ono made a token appearance at the film studio late in the afternoon, reverting to type as contemptuous truants.

In their absence, McCartney, Linda Eastman, Starr, and Neil Aspinall discussed the group's internal politics, revealing that the meeting had ended in a provisional, noncommittal agreement that the group should split up—but not immediately. Discussion seems to have been cut short by Harrison's (quite reasonable) refusal to allow Yoko Ono a voice in deciding the group's future. As Lennon insisted she should be present, communications quickly broke down, and the meeting was abandoned.

Now, at Twickenham, McCartney was prepared to go further than ever before in criticizing Lennon's attitude—albeit when he wasn't present. He deplored Ono's hold over his songwriting partner, and indirectly observed that, by this stage, Harrison's disagreements with Lennon were much stronger than any musical disputes he'd endured with McCartney. He noted that it would be ironic if the Beatles were to break up merely because Lennon insisted on bringing his girlfriend to their sessions. And he concluded that if their internal chaos was not righted by the end of the week, the day before they were due to play their show, then they should split up, finally and definitively. Given the candid nature of their discussion, it's somehow appropriate that when Lennon did show his face, McCartney dragooned him into an ineffectual rehearsal of "Get Back."

On 14 January, the Beatles endured the same charade. This time, the Lennons arrived at the same time as actor Peter Sellers, who was afforded the opportunity to play straight man to a burst of Lennonesque drug chic. "Showbiz people need a form of relaxation," John declared. "It's that or exercise, and drugs win hands down." "Shooting [heroin] is exercise," added Yoko delightedly. Otherwise, the day delivered nothing more concrete than a lengthy Lennon/McCartney/Starr improvisation around two Lennon fragments, "Madman" and "Watching Rainbows."

There were now four days to go until Michael Lindsay-Hogg was scheduled to film the Beatles in concert. Not even the most utopian of Apple employees was convinced that the show would take place on time, and the long-suffering Derek Taylor was deputed to brief the press that the date had been postponed because the Beatles "weren't ready."

Behind the scenes, Taylor was performing a more arduous, and important, task. "It was unbearable to me that they should break up," he wrote in his autobiography, *Fifty Years Adrift.* "Brian Epstein, I knew, would have fought and fought to keep them together; and so, when the four of them met at Apple after George's walk-out, I was bolder than I had ever been or ever would be again and demanded that George not let Paul carry the weight of keeping the film and the Beatles going. I felt that George's sense of decency could be touched, and it was: he returned, and the film was completed." His reward, less than a week later, was a postcard from Paul McCartney. The stamp bearing the queen's head was torn in two, and the message was brief, and unmistakable: "Up yer."

That meeting at Apple took place on 15 January, five days after Harrison's decision to leave the group, and it resulted in a complete rethink of the movie project. For a start, all four Beatles were anxious to escape from Twickenham and its soulless ambience. Instead, the group elected to reconvene after the weekend, on 20 January, at their own newly constructed Apple studio, in the basement of their plush headquarters at 3 Savile Row in London's West End.

Jettisoned with the Twickenham location was the live concert, the trigger that had originally set the film in motion. But despite their lack of progress to date, the Beatles were still collectively enthusiastic about recording a new album with a minimum of overdubs and studio trickery. Lindsay-Hogg was duly briefed that his concert film had now become a documentary about the making of the next Beatles record.

Briefly, harmony reigned within the group, although it is fascinating to speculate what might have happened had the meeting taken place some twenty-four hours later. By then, the new issue of the British pop weekly *Disc and Music Echo* had reached the street, trumpeting a typically indiscreet interview with John Lennon in which he announced that Apple was running at a dramatic loss, and that the Beatles were in imminent danger of bankruptcy unless the tide could be turned.

"We had one hundred fifty people working there," Ringo claimed to *Melody Maker* in 1971, by which time both Apple's staff and its ideals had been trimmed down to size. "We had a ninety-quid booze bill every week, 'cos we were crazed. We're not businessmen. We played at it, and so suddenly we had a thousand people that weren't needed. But they all enjoyed it; they're all getting paid to sit around. We had a guy there to read the Tarot cards, or to read the *I Ching*. It was craziness, and we suddenly realised the craziness—that it's not a business, that nothing's getting done, we have a million people and what's getting done? So we cut it down, and you cut it down until it's working, and now it functions. It's like pruning the tree. If you have a big tree with a thousand million rose bushes, you get little roses. Prune it down and you might get ten fantastic roses."

Ringo Starr's version of Reaganomics was totally at odds with the Beatles' original vision of Apple as "a kind of Western Communism." But their image of utopia was undeniably tarnished when they gathered at Apple Studios on 20 January, ready to resume work.

The construction and completion of the studio had been left in the hands of Apple's in-house electronics wizard, "Magic" Alex Mardas. "Alex's recording studio was the biggest disaster of all time," George Harrison remembered in *I Me Mine.* "He was walking around with a white coat on like some sort of chemist, but he didn't have a clue what he was doing. It was a sixteen-track system, and he had sixteen tiny little speakers all around the walls. You only need two speakers for stereo sound. It was awful. The whole thing was a disaster, and it had to be ripped out."

George Martin and Glyn Johns were given two days to transform Apple from an experimental nightmare into a passable approximation of a professional recording studio. They brought in a mobile console and mixing desk, managed to silence the heating and air conditioning system that would otherwise have infiltrated every take, and overhauled the sound-proofing.

Twenty days after they'd first jammed at Twickenham, the Beatles resumed work at Apple—once more under the gaze of Michael Lindsay-Hogg's camera crew. This time, they were also being documented on EMI's eight-track recording tape, as well as the Nagra audio sync for the film footage. As at any other Beatles session, the producer (usually George Martin, but sometimes Glyn Johns) only switched on the recording console when the group announced they were ready for a take; meanwhile, their false starts, stumbles, and conversation continued to register on Lindsay-Hogg's machines.

The initial session at Apple, an altogether more intimate setting than the vast aircraft hangar at Twickenham, proved more productive than they might have expected. Though they continued to debate the fine points of an arrangement for "I've Got a Feeling," the discussion was even-tempered, even cooperative. After calling for a cymbal crash from Ringo, "to give me the courage to come screaming in," Lennon delivered an intense take of "Don't Let Me Down," captured for posterity by Glyn Johns.

Lennon also spent some time guiding the band through the twists and turns of "Dig a Pony," admitting that his various sets of lyrics for the song were interchangeable. In one of the most revealing episodes of the band's entire career, Paul McCartney read out a savage attack on the Beatles from the previous day's issue of the London *Daily Sketch,* while the other Beatles jammed along in support. "The awful tension of being locked in each other's arms snapped last night at TV rehearsal," McCartney intoned in a parody of a broadcaster's voice. "Drugs, divorce and a slipping image played desperately on their minds, and it appeared to them all that the public was being encouraged to hate them. . . . They will probably never be the same again."

Any danger that the Apple sessions would prove as unproductive as the Twickenham fiasco vanished on the first afternoon, when a fifth musician entered the studio. The Beatles had first met keyboardist Billy Preston when he'd toured Britain in Little Richard's band back in 1962, and as keen followers of the American soul scene, they were doubtless familiar with the R&B instrumentals he'd released as a soloist since then. Harrison had renewed the acquaintance the previous year, when Preston was back in Britain with Ray Charles's soul revue, and invited the American to pay him a visit at Apple.

Preston turned up, apparently without warning, early in the afternoon of 22 January, whereupon Harrison whisked him downstairs to the basement studio, where he proceeded to flesh out the rehearsals of "She Came in through the Bathroom Window," "I've Got a Feeling," and "Don't Let Me Down." At the end of the session, Lennon made a unilateral decision: "Why don't you be on the album? Every number's got a piano part. Normally, we overdub it, but this time we want to do it live. Live to ourselves." For the next nine days, much to Paul McCartney's initial chagrin, there were now five Beatles.

The question of Billy Preston's status was raised early on 24 January. McCartney was obviously wary of placing an obstacle in the way of Lennon and Harrison's vocal enthusiasm for their new recruit, so he could only approach the subject obliquely. "I think he is more like Ray Charles, an album artist," he ventured, suggesting that he was too much of a jazz player to fit into the Beatles' style.

"Billy is so knocked out," Harrison countered, all the Twickenham cynicism vanished from his voice. "He's just thrilled. He sees it as a great opportunity."

"I see it as ours, too," added Lennon. "I'd like him in our band, actually. I'd like a fifth Beatle."

"It's bad enough with four!" McCartney replied. "But with five, and a spade, it's creating havoc. You know, I dig him. He's an incredible musician. But he was only sitting in until I said, [adopts stage voice] 'Billy Preston, you're on the show.'" (The reference to Preston's being a "spade" was not indicative of any racial prejudice on McCartney's part; it was common parlance among "hip" British musicians in the late '60s, and carried no aura of insult. If anyone was going to be put out, it would have been Harrison and Lennon, who had actually invited Preston to participate.)

Meanwhile, there was an album to finish. "Are we making a record now?" asked a confused Ringo Starr during the session. "No, we're still rehearsing," McCartney explained patiently. "'Get Back' is the only song we've got . . ."

"I think we've got 'Don't Let Me Down' and 'Dig a Pony,' actually," Lennon interjected. "Dig a Pony" was taped by Glyn Johns that afternoon, as were "I've Got a Feeling" and a lengthy rehearsal session in which McCartney taught the others a whimsical number called "Teddy Boy." Lennon promptly satirized it as a square dance, an episode so damning that it's remarkable Johns considered it worth including on the (aborted) *Get Back* LP.

Having survived nearly a week at Apple without complaint, Harrison now moaned that "the film is becoming very boring." But at least, with the tape machines rolling intermittently, the Beatles were progressing toward a recognizable destination. Anxious to capitalize on this tenuous harmony, the group elected to cancel their weekend off and carry on working.

Glyn Johns also put in some overtime on the evening of 24 January. "I mixed a bunch of stuff that they didn't even know I'd recorded, half the time," he recalled a decade later in *The Record Producers*. "I just whacked the recorder on for a lot of stuff that they did, and gave them an acetate the following morning of what I'd done, as a rough idea of what an album could be like . . . that became an obsession with me."

The following day, as Johns explained, "They came back and said they didn't like it, and that was the end of that." But the opportunity to judge their rate of progress allowed the Beatles some much needed perspective on their work. On 25 January, "Two of Us" took coherent shape as a semiacoustic song, the way Johns had suggested at Twickenham. Harrison persuaded the band to reconsider "For You Blue," with Lennon donning a thumb pick and making a commendable stab at mastering the lap-steel guitar. "Let It Be" also neared completion, albeit at the expense of Lennon's and Harrison's patience. Both musicians showed signs of weariness by the end of the day.

On Sunday, they briefly toyed with Ringo's "Octopus's Garden," before choosing to set it aside. But Lindsay-Hogg's crew did capture two of the most exhilarating moments in the movie. The first was a raucous rock 'n' roll jam, which was almost professional, and led from "Shake, Rattle, and Roll" through elements of the Little Richard back catalog to "Blue Suede Shoes," and finally a deliciously ramshackle revival of the Miracles' "You Really Got a Hold on Me." The second was "Dig It," another of the Beatles' improvised jams, enlivened by the presence of Billy Preston and by the fact that this time—unlike at Twickenham—wasn't an excuse for Lennon and McCartney to avoid having to work on a Harrison song. The full jam ran for eight minutes or more, and its impromptu appeal was so obvious to all concerned that places were immediately reserved for it in the documentary film and on the accompanying album. Everything played that day had a built-in sense of fun, whether McCartney was reprising Jimmy McCracklin's sinuous blues, "The Walk," or yielding the microphone to Linda Eastman's daughter, Heather, for a charmingly naive improvisation.

As the material slowly congealed into something approaching cogent songs, Paul McCartney dared to revive the taboo subject of the live show.

"We still haven't got any aim for what we're doing now, except an album again," he explained gently to the others on 29 January. "Our only aim is an album, which is a very nonvisual thing. I really think we can be into other things, but every time I talk about it I really sound like I'm the show-biz correspondent trying to hustle us to do a Judy Garland comeback."

While the others continued to respond with silence, McCartney ventured a little further: "We really have to want to do a show at the end of it. I'd love to do that, just to play all these numbers one afternoon at the Savile [Theatre] to some people. Then we could do a couple of other small shows until we hit it and get over our nervousness with an audience."

McCartney's suggestion was that they should take advantage of the fact that they had, at last, around half a dozen songs they could perform with some proficiency. Instead of constantly rescheduling a live concert into a disappearing future, why not do the show right now?

Surprisingly, it was Lennon who responded most enthusiastically to the idea. "I think it would be daft of us not to play tomorrow," he explained, "even if it's a grand dress rehearsal. Let's see how it goes, let's look at how we look, look at the rushes of the seven songs." When Michael Lindsay-Hogg complained that "at the moment, this documentary's like [Jean-Paul Sartre's] No Exit . . . there's lot of good footage, but no pay-off," even Harrison concurred: "We should film it while we're recording, but let's get it done."

At lunchtime on 30 January 1969, the Beatles prepared for their final public performance: on top of their Savile Row headquarters, staring out across the rooftops of London's West End. Suggested as a convenient venue by Glyn Johns, the Apple roof wasn't quite the exotic location that Lindsay-Hogg had been hoping for. But it was outdoors, as McCartney had suggested, and at least the logistics were simple: Apple staff merely had to carry the group's instruments and amps up from the basement.

Cameramen balanced precariously on the edge of the flat roof, while a small group of wives and Apple insiders snuggled against a chimney stack. Clad in thick winter coats, the four Beatles and Billy Preston tried to adjust to the cutting chill of a midwinter wind.

For the next forty minutes, they struggled to keep their fingers warm and their voices clear, as they performed a selection of the more raucous material they'd been rehearsing over the previous four weeks. Yoko Ono

must have been delighted: their audience was mostly invisible. The spectators weren't quite as conceptual as she would have preferred, though, merely craning their necks up to the sky in a vain attempt to identify what might be former teen idols blasting their songs at concert volume across the London skyline.

They began with a fiery but erratic "Get Back," after which Michael Lindsay-Hogg demanded more volume from engineer Glyn Johns, and John Lennon ventured the first of a series of mock stage announcements: "We've had a request from Martin and Luther." A second "Get Back" was sprightly enough to make the *Let It Be* movie, as was a gloriously sprawling version of "Don't Let Me Down," complete with Lennon's collapse into gibberish as he missed the start of the second verse. With the Lennon/McCartney partnership renewing its camaraderie in the open air,

THE ALBUMS

only Harrison was cast in the role of skeptic, rarely attempting eye contact with any of his colleagues.

Their best rendition of "I've Got a Feeling" to date ensured its inclusion in both the film and on the soundtrack album, and the Beatles romped through "The One after 909" with all the carefree joy of their adolescent days at the Top Ten Club in Hamburg almost a decade earlier. "Dig a Pony" concluded a run of three superb performances, all of which were preserved on record and celluloid.

Thereafter, relief that they'd mastered the day's repertoire took its toll. Instrumental precision was also hampered by the elements. "My hands are getting too cold to play the chords," Lennon complained after "Dig a Pony." The day's second attempt at "I've Got a Feeling" was lackluster, dissolving into boredom once everyone in the band realized that this take wasn't the one. "I've got a feeling that we've done it before," Harrison sang as it trailed to a halt.

George was keen to lead the band into their final number, a reprise of "Get Back," but Lindsay-Hogg demanded a second "Don't Let Me Down," which was rendered unusable when Lennon again forgot the lyrics. Then came the third and last "Get Back"—which was transformed into an exquisite piece of theater by an intervention that McCartney might have prayed for, but could never have planned. Alerted by local businessmen that very strange noises were emanating from the rooftop at 3 Savile Row, the Metropolitan Police marched into Apple headquarters and demanded a halt to the performance. Gaining access to the roof, they instructed roadie Mal Evans to switch off the amplifiers. Suddenly, only McCartney and Starr were audible, until a visibly annoyed Harrison flicked back the switches and the group was restored to full, chaotic volume.

As the last Beatles live performance careened to an end, McCartney improvised some lines about naughty boys being arrested for playing on roofs. Maureen Starkey led the applause, prompting a final one-liner from Lennon: "On behalf of the group and ourselves, I hope we passed the audition." It was a perfect ending for the film and the soundtrack album.

But it wasn't quite the end of the sessions. The next day, in an altogether more sober mood, the Beatles gathered in Apple's basement studio, where they reeled off take after take of the three most delicate songs they'd sought to master that month: "Two of Us," "Let It Be," and "The Long and Winding Road." While Paul gazed soulfully at Lindsay-Hogg's

cameras as he crooned his piano ballads, John picked almost incoherent lines on his adopted instrument for the day, the bass guitar. "The Long and Winding Road" suffered most from his inability to maintain tempo and key. But the Beatles had long since abandoned any hope of perfection, and after four tortuous weeks it was a wrap. For (in Lennon's phrase) the group and themselves—rapidly becoming two separate entities—it was time to wake up from the nightmare of January 1969. Another dark night, though, was about to overcome them.

In New York, one man was particularly intrigued by John Lennon's public admission that the Beatles were running short of cash. As manager of both the Rolling Stones and Donovan, Allen Klein was hardly unknown to the Beatles; in fact, they'd been wary of his unscrupulous reputation since learning years earlier that he'd vowed to add the Beatles to his artist roster.

During the gap between completion of *The White Album* and the commencement of filming, Lennon and McCartney had begun scouting around for a potential financial savior. They'd consulted Lord Beeching, a British politician best remembered for his savage cost-cutting assaults on the national railway system in the early '60s. Beeching had offered to advise the Beatles on how to streamline their Apple operation, but his conservative outlook was scarcely designed to appeal to Lennon.

Klein was something else. During the final week of film sessions at Apple, the New Yorker approached John Lennon, suggesting an informal meeting to discuss the Beatles' business arrangements. After checking with Mick Jagger and Donovan that he would emerge from the meeting with his shirt intact, Lennon agreed to see Klein on 28 January. "He can take over everything," Derek Taylor remembers hearing him say on his return. "He's great, incredible."

Harrison and Starr were quickly swayed by Lennon's naive enthusiasm, but McCartney had gently been lobbying the group to accept assistance from Lee Eastman, father of his girlfriend, Linda. For the moment, a compromise was reached. On 3 February 1969, three days after the close of filming, it was announced that "the Beatles have asked Mr Klein to look into all their affairs, and he has agreed to do so." The following day, Lee Eastman was appointed to advise the group on all their legal affairs. The friction between the sharp-talking, bearlike Klein and the genteel, fastidious Eastman quickly divided Lennon and McCartney into rival camps; the resulting intrigue bedeviled the Beatles' final year as an active group.

"I can be conned quite easily," Lennon admitted to Peter McCabe and Robert Schonfeld after the group split. "But it's not easy to get through all the defenses and see what I'm like. Klein knew me quite well, without even meeting me. Also he knew to come to me and not to go to Paul, whereas someone like Lew Grade or Eastman would have gone to Paul."

The unholy alliance of Klein, Eastman, and the Beatles immediately instigated a campaign to win control of NEMS Enterprises, the company through which Brian Epstein had managed the group and which had now passed into the hands of Epstein's brother, Clive. The financial group

Triumph Investments was negotiating a takeover of NEMS with Clive Epstein; Klein and Eastman were instructed to construct a rival bid and prevent NEMS from falling into "foreign," or at least unfamiliar, hands.

The financial complications stalled any further work on the film, or the album, and matters were delayed again when George Harrison was hospitalized with severe tonsillitis. Even so, Apple was officially upbeat about the prospects for the album: twelve tracks were announced as completed by the end of January, and just four more songs, it was claimed, needed additional work before the April 1969 release date could be met.

With that in mind, the Beatles regrouped at another unfamiliar location, Trident Studios in Soho, on 22 and 23 February, to recommence work on a number they'd toyed with during one of the Apple sessions: Lennon's "I Want You (She's So Heavy)." But after two days of work, the song was set aside and no further sessions were scheduled.

At some stage between 23 February and early March, the Beatles agreed that they could no longer stomach the idea of adding further material to their January stockpile. Instead, Lennon and McCartney summoned recording engineer Glyn Johns to a meeting at Abbey Road, where they handed over the Apple tapes from 22 to 31 January and requested that he turn them into a credible album. "They pointed to a big pile of tapes in the corner," the engineer recalled in *The Record Producers,* "and said, 'Remember that idea you had about putting together an album? Well, there are the tapes. Go and do it.'"

Johns admitted that he was "absolutely petrified" by the responsibility, but he approached this thankless task with initial enthusiasm, reviewing the tapes, cataloging them in terms of their potential value, and then booking Olympic Studios in Barnes for a week in mid-March so he could prepare rough mixes of the best material. As he began work, the Apple publicity machine geared up for an imminent release. The four "extra" tracks promised in February were forgotten, and Apple was now pledging that the album would include just twelve tracks.

Johns must have been amused by some of their other claims—like the statement that "around two dozen tracks have been completed and are ready for release," or the proud boast that these included "Maxwell's Silver Hammer" (abandoned because of boredom during the January sessions), "Polythene Pam" (scrapped because Lennon hadn't finished writing it) and "Octopus's Garden" (written, but never actually performed by the Beatles during the sessions). Apple's statement entered further realms of fantasy when the company's press spokesman announced that the January sessions had also spawned rerecordings of three songs left over from the *White Album* sessions: Harrison's "Not Guilty," Lennon's "What's the New Mary Jane," and McCartney's "Jubilee." "Let me have them, then," Glyn Johns must have muttered in his Olympic hideaway.

For another month, there was no public statement of progress, though the Beatles weren't exactly out of the news. During that time, both Lennon and McCartney were married, Harrison was busted for possession of marijuana, and Lennon and his wife, Yoko Ono, staged their honeymoon in front of the world's press as part of an ongoing campaign calling for universal peace. Amid those headlines, no one was looking too hard for more news about "Polythene Pam."

That was just as well. During his week at Olympic Studios, Glyn Johns had isolated a batch of recordings that could just about be dragged into shape as an album—albeit an uninspired one. Rescued from the January tapes were precisely ten original songs: "Get Back," "Dig It," "Teddy Boy," "Two of Us (On Our Way Home)," "Dig a Pony," "I've Got a Feeling," "The Long and Winding Road," "Let It Be," "Don't Let Me Down," and "Because You're Sweet and Lovely Girl" (alias "For You Blue").

In an effort to extend these to fill a twelve-track album, Johns also mixed a brief instrumental he called "Rocker" and a rousing romp through the traditional Liverpool folk tune "Maggie Mae," plus impromptu renditions of a set of rock 'n' roll oldies: "The Walk," "Save the Last Dance for Me," "Shake, Rattle, and Roll," "Kansas City," "Miss Ann," "Lawdy Miss Clawdy," "Blue Suede Shoes," and "You Really Got a Hold on Me."

The engineer's choice of takes often verged on the inexplicable. For instance, he ignored the near-perfect takes of "Two of Us" and "Let It Be" secured on 31 January in favor of earlier, more erratic run-throughs. Presumably following instructions from the Beatles, he completely ignored the tapes of the 30 January rooftop session. His preferred version of "I've Got a Feeling" didn't so much end as collapse. "Teddy Boy" was left virtually intact, highlighting the fact that it was a six-minute illustration of McCartney boring the rest of the group into sarcasm. Glyn Johns's pick of the "best" takes of "Don't Let Me Down" and "Two of Us" was also open to question. A tape of his first acetate mix, completed on 10 March, leaked to American radio stations six months later—the same week, coincidentally, that Apple sent out promotional copies of *Abbey Road*. Reviewing the results between their marital commitments, the Beatles identified two facts: the album would be a disaster, and as they'd suspected from the start, "Get Back" would make a great single.

While Lennon and Ono were in bed in Amsterdam, EMI engineers were remixing "Get Back," which was okayed by the Beatles before being sent to BBC Radio 1 for prerelease airing on 6 April. McCartney monitored the broadcasts, then pronounced himself dissatisfied with the mix, and the following day—four days before the single reached the shops—he and Glyn Johns prepared a final version for release.

McCartney's hand was also evident in the press adverts for the single: "'Get Back' is the Beatles' new single. It's the first Beatles record which is as live as can be, in this electronic age. There's no electronic whatchamacallit. 'Get Back' is a pure spring-time rock number. On the other side there's an equally live number called 'Don't Let Me Down.'

"Paul's got this to say about 'Get Back' . . . 'we were sitting in the studio and we made it up out of thin air . . . we started to write words there and then . . . when we finished it, we recorded it at Apple Studios and made it into a song to roller-coast by.'

"P.S. John adds, It's John playing the fab live guitar solo. And now John on 'Don't Let Me Down': John says don't let me down about 'Don't Let Me Down.'

"In 'Get Back' and 'Don't Let Me Down,' you'll find the Beatles, as nature intended."

A worldwide No. 1, "Get Back" was accepted at face value, as a conscious return to the Beatles' rock 'n' roll roots and a positive harbinger of the forthcoming album. Squeezing something out of their January sessions seems to have lightened the Beatles' mood. Three days after "Get Back" was released, Lennon and McCartney taped a follow-up single, "The Ballad of John and Yoko," which was released at the end of May.

More to the point, sessions resumed in mid-April for a Beatles album, though no one was still quite sure what form this would take. "I

**Facing the truth. George,
Ringo, Yoko, John, Paul.**
Courtesy of Photofest

Want You (She's So Heavy)" was the first song to be approached, before
the group took their first serious stab at Harrison's "Something."

Interviewed by *Disc* at this point, Lennon was decidedly upbeat: "If
I could only get the time to myself, I think I could probably write about 30
songs a day. As it is, I probably average about 12 a night. Paul, too: he's
mad on it. As soon as I leave here, I'm going round to Paul's place and
we'll sit down and start work.

"The way we're writing at the moment," Lennon continued, "it's
straightforward and there's nothing weird. The songs are like 'Get Back.'
A lot of the tracks on the next LP will be like 'Get Back,' and a lot of that
we did in one take. We've done about twelve tracks, some of them still to
be remixed. All the songs we're doing sound normal to me, but probably
they might sound unusual to you. There's no 'Revolution #9' there—but
there's a few heavy sounds."

Amid the beneficent hype, Lennon let slip to the *New Musical Express* a hint that something beyond a soundtrack of their January sessions was under way: "Paul and I are now working on a kind of song montage that we might do as one piece on one side. We've got about two weeks to finish the whole thing, so we're really working at it." In retrospect, this statement is remarkable for two reasons. First, it dates from around 20 April, fully two weeks before the Beatles attempted any of the songs that ended up on the *Abbey Road* side 2 "medley." Second, it shows that the "medley" was a joint venture from the start. Twenty years after the event, George Martin told BBC DJ Spencer Leigh, "The symphonic piece on Side 2 (of *Abbey Road*) was my idea, and to be quite honest, John didn't approve." Lennon himself repeatedly damned the "medley" as a McCartney invention, claiming that he'd wanted no part of it from the start. But in April 1969, Lennon was not only taking cocredit for the project but also suggesting that it might be slipped onto an otherwise audio vérité album from the January sessions.

The fact that the medley was already clearly defined by late April is confirmed by Chris Thomas, who in the absence of George Martin had acted as the Beatles' producer on several occasions over the previous year: "When it came to *Let It Be,* I didn't go down to many of those sessions, I never went to Twickenham at all, then they sort of petered out and they went back to Abbey Road and everything seemed to meander along. Then they started doing more new stuff and that sort of became *Abbey Road* . . . [but] I remember Paul sitting down in Abbey Road No. 3 and playing me this whole thing which lasted about fifteen minutes, it goes into this and into that."

The medley was both an admission that the group was light on weighty new material and a conceptual breakthrough. Typically, the Beatles were borrowing an idea from showbiz, filtered through the rock underground. Medleys were the stock-in-trade of cabaret singers and big bands and a standard device in stage or movie musicals.

The tactic of segueing compositions together had also become familiar in left-field rock circles. Artists like Frank Zappa, Jefferson Airplane, and Soft Machine utilized seamless transitions to avoid the restrictions of the song format. Whether the initial idea was Lennon's or McCartney's, it bore the latter's trademark: throughout his "experimental" period, from 1965 through the end of the decade, McCartney was often treated as an innovator for simply twisting avant-garde techniques into a shape that could be assimilated by a mass audience. It had proved to be a key ingredient in the Beatles' latter-day musical development.

From mid-April until the first week of May, the group worked as a unit on several of the songs destined for *Abbey Road:* "Octopus's Garden," "Oh! Darling," and "You Never Give Me Your Money." All these songs were developed in the studio, but their basic structure remained unaltered from start to finish. Even the lengthy medleys seem to have arrived at the sessions fully formed. By simply documenting the songs, not revamping them, the Beatles had cleverly eliminated a potential area of strife.

Even while work was continuing on the new songs, the group couldn't resist tinkering with the January tapes. Harrison overdubbed a guitar solo onto "Let It Be," thereby perverting the "live" aesthetic of the original recording, while Glyn Johns assembled spoken-word snippets to slot between the January tracks.

"It was all done like a rehearsal," Lennon gushed to the *New Musical Express* as he looked forward to the release of the Glyn Johns album. "Only one track got finished, and that was 'Get Back.' The others are in various stages of completion. One day, we just decided to stop right away, or we'd be doing another of those four-month numbers." The LP's title, he announced, would be *Get Back, Don't Let Me Down, and Twelve Other Songs,* and the cover would be "just like *Please Please Me.* We had our picture taken in the same positions as on that early album, but looking like we do now. It's great."

The final recording session undertaken by the Beatles before they agreed to take a spring recess for their solo commitments took place on 6 May 1969. Glyn Johns was left to assemble the *Get Back, Don't Let Me Down* LP. It was another two months before they resumed studio work, by which time the temporary rapprochement in group relations, which had been maintained since March, had broken down irrevocably.

"The split was over Klein and Eastman," John Lennon stated baldly the year after the Beatles' dissolution became public. Derek Taylor, apt to refer to Allen Klein as the Demon King of myth, assumed some of the guilt for his appointment as the group's manager (in *Fifty Years Adrift*): "Klein had first come to call at his own suggestion, but it was I who suggested, in the light of the Fabnesses' despair, that they determine whether the reputed coldness of his methods outweighed his undoubted capacity for securing the greatest of deals for his clients . . . John was desperate with confusion, and saw so much money pouring out of Apple that this new wizard, Magic Allen, must have seemed to him like the Saviour."

Klein's radical cost-cutting entailed the loss of many key Apple personnel, some of whom had been working for the Beatles since their initial rise to fame. It was ironic that the most utopian member of the group should now be the keenest supporter of Klein's hard-edged financial realism. But the New Yorker's primary functions, as far as all of the group was concerned, were to renegotiate their recording contract with EMI (still bringing them laughably low royalty rates) and to counter the twin assaults being mounted against the group's corporate assets.

The first battle was quickly lost, and then discounted. Though the Beatles wanted to retain a controlling stake in the Epsteins' NEMS Enterprises, they were outmaneuvered in February by Triumph Investments. No sooner had Linda Eastman's brother John written to Clive Epstein demanding a summit than Epstein sold out 70 percent of NEMS' holding company to Triumph. Klein must have relished this exhibition of Eastman powerlessness, and by the end of February he'd severed links between the Beatles and NEMS, insisting that EMI should pay all future royalties directly to the group—or, as soon became apparent, directly via Allen Klein.

The second conflict was more personal, especially for Lennon and McCartney. Music publisher Dick James had formed Northern Songs as a vehicle for Lennon/McCartney material early in 1963, and had become a millionaire as a result. The Beatles' initial respect for the man who guarded their songwriting rights was gradually supplanted by dry amusement, as James turned up at their recording sessions anxious to hear another hit, and finally deepening resentment. In the summer of 1968, an Apple film crew documented a sarcastic exchange between Lennon and James, the singer leaving his publisher in no doubt that only legal red tape was keeping their relationship intact.

The bonds of loyalty were stretched on both sides, and in early March 1969 Dick James—no doubt aware that increased tension among the group was threatening their future—offered to sell his 37.5 percent of stock in Northern Songs to the legendary British impresario and businessman Sir Lew Grade of ATV. Ironically, Grade was one of those whom the Beatles had already canvassed for advice about Apple's precarious financial standing.

ATV clinched the deal in mid-March, while Lennon and McCartney were distracted by their respective weddings. But Lennon returned from his Amsterdam bed-in with Yoko to attend a meeting on 1 April with Klein and McCartney, in which they discussed how to use their joint 29.7 percent of Northern Songs shares to prevent a total takeover of the company by ATV. Grade immediately offered to buy out Lennon and McCartney; the Beatles made a counteroffer to the individuals and institutions who controlled the remaining, crucial Northern stock.

For the next seven weeks, Lennon's attention was divided between his burgeoning campaign for world peace and his bitter struggle to keep hold of the company that owned his and McCartney's songs. In public, John was sending world leaders acorns, which might grow into oak trees symbolizing universal goodwill and understanding. In private, he was aiming vitriolic barbs at James, Grade, and the entire race of "fat businessmen sitting on their asses in the city."

The battle for Northern Songs was the final campaign waged by the team of John Lennon and Paul McCartney. Lennon, at least, relished the primitive aggression of the struggle: "It was fantastic," he told *Rolling Stone.* "It was like this room full of old men, smoking and fighting, deciding. It's great. Businessmen play the game the way we play music, and it's something to see."

McCartney was less aroused by the spectacle. He steered his reactions into the melancholy, resigned lyrics of the song the Beatles began recording at the height of the dispute. "You never give me your money," he wrote, "you only give me your funny paper. And in the middle of negotiations, I break down."

And so, slowly and inevitably, did the unity of the Lennon/McCartney partnership. "We were together every day for these terrible, terrible meetings which made us uptight," Lennon confirmed to the *New Musical Express* at the end of the year. "It's all that [stuff] that's still in the air between us. It was so hard for us. We had to listen to all this jazz about business, and about banking, and try to think about the technicalities.

"We got to hear how much we'd wasted, and that was a real bringdown. It put all of us in the Beatles into the wrong situation. God, I don't like to think about the money we wasted. It was such a waste. I'd rather have given it away to some deserving gypsy." Instead, final control of Northern Songs was transferred in mid-May, when the minority, neutral shareholders accepted ATV's offer of a lucrative buyout. Lennon and McCartney were marooned, destined to remain in eternal opposition to Grade's monolithic control.

Although Klein and Eastman—Lennon and McCartney—had lined up on the same side of the barricades for the duration of the campaign, each of the rival factions figured that with more support from the other, their team might have ended up victorious. McCartney's marriage into the Eastman family stifled his sympathy for the earthier tactics employed by Klein. Lee and John Eastman recounted tales of what they viewed as Klein's underhand methods in previous legal disputes; meanwhile, Lennon relished every speck of dirt covering his man's reputation.

"Allen's human," he told a reporter at the height of his obsession with the New Yorker. "Eastman and all them other people are automatons." What evidence could he offer in Klein's defense? Emotional solidarity: "Allen's one of the lads. I would go on holiday with him, he pisses about. When he and his crew go on tour, they piss about like schoolkids, pretending to be deaf and dumb, whatever kind of crazy thing. He's good fun to be around."

McCartney might have accepted Lennon's imitations of "cripples" during the Beatles' mid-'60s concerts, but he expected something more sober from their manager. On 8 May, two days after they began work on "You Never Give Me Your Money," the Beatles appointed Allen Klein as the business manager of Apple Corps Ltd.—and hence of the group itself. However, McCartney never signed the contract, and henceforth refused

Paul pondering fate.

to accept Klein's jurisdiction over his affairs. His relationship with Lennon was never the same again.

For the next seven weeks, Lennon and McCartney met only in the company of business suits and "fat asses," as the sands of their rescue bid for Northern Songs slipped away. Then Lennon flew to Canada, to begin another bed-in, during which he recorded his first solo single with the Plastic Ono Band, "Give Peace a Chance." Out of habit more than love, John credited the song to Lennon/McCartney. "It should have been Lennon/Ono," he admitted to *Playboy* shortly before his death.

At the end of May, while the Lennons were in Toronto and the McCartneys on holiday in the United States, Glyn Johns delivered his completed version of the Beatles' next LP, *Get Back, Don't Let Me Down, and Twelve Other Songs.* "We didn't want to know," Lennon explained to *Rolling Stone.* "We just left it to him and said, 'Here, do it.' It was the first time since our first album that we didn't have anything to do with it. None of us could be bothered going in—Paul, nobody. Nobody called anybody about it, and the tapes were left there. We got an acetate each and we called each other and said, 'What do you think? Oh, let it out.'

"We were going to let it out in really shitty condition. I didn't care. I thought it was good to let it out and show people what had happened to us. 'This is where we're at now, we can't get it together, we don't play together anymore, leave us alone.' But that didn't happen."

It was obvious why it didn't happen. Though Johns had replaced the versions of "Let It Be" and "Get Back" that he'd originally chosen, his track selection repeated most of the follies of his initial acetate in March (see Discography for details of the tracks selected). In this state, *Get Back* was certainly an accurate reflection of the January sessions, right down to the fragmentary, faltering stroll through the Drifters' "Save the Last Dance for Me" and the joyous romp through "Dig It." But its programming was suspect, to say the least. Setting "Let It Be" and "The Long and Winding Road" back-to-back at the end of the second side was certainly an unusual piece of sequencing, especially as they were followed by an off-cut from the LP's title track that seemed to depict McCartney laughing at his own solemnity.

For all its failings, the *Get Back* LP might—just might—have been accepted as the soundtrack to a film. But Michael Lindsay-Hogg's movie had reached stasis. Apple announced proudly that sixty-eight hours of footage had now been edited down to five, or maybe two, and that a rough cut was being assembled for the benefit of TV buyers. Meanwhile, Jonathan Cott and David Dalton were working on the text for the accompanying book about the sessions. But the Beatles' refusal to sanction the immediate release of the tie-in album left the project in limbo.

With *Get Back* perished two other plans, both of which had been optimistically tossed around the group since the January sessions. Personal communication within the Beatles was now proving to be well-nigh impossible. So Lennon, Harrison, and Starr carried on a media debate in the spring of 1969 about the benefits (or otherwise) of the very thing that Paul McCartney had spent the whole of January trying to sell them on: live concerts.

During his honeymoon in March, Lennon told the gathered reporters that "The Beatles will give several public shows this year." The news was wired back to London, where Ringo Starr had just informed the *New Musical Express* that "personally, I don't want to play in public again. I just don't want to do it." What was more, Ringo said he didn't "miss being a Beatle anymore. You can't get those days back. It's no good living in the past." A beleaguered Apple spokesman was reduced to the guarded language of the diplomatic corps: "It would be indelicate for us to comment whilst John and Ringo are so obviously in disagreement."

George Harrison hoped to appease both sides: "Maybe after the first show, I'd want to do it all again, maybe go on tour, do the lot. I really don't know." McCartney maintained a dignified, but presumably pained, silence. As usual, silence wasn't an option for Lennon. "I quite fancy giving some live shows," he insisted to the *New Musical Express* in April, "but I can't give you any definite plans when we're not even agreed on it. There's too much going on now for us to even talk realistically about going on tour. In a way, that's why it's unfortunate that all the publicity came out about doing live shows when it did. We were only thinking about it vaguely, but it kind of got out of hand."

Upon that vagueness the destiny of the Beatles was sealed. Without McCartney interpreting Lennon's silence months earlier as tacit agreement, there would have been no promise of a December show at the Royal Albert Hall, no dealings with the Roundhouse, no Twickenham Studios, no Michael Lindsay-Hogg, no *Get Back,* no *Let It Be* . . . no wonder McCartney kept his head down. Not Lennon, though, who followed up on his avowed enthusiasm for touring in another *New Musical Express* interview two weeks later, in which he stated that "I think Ringo was right about not touring. The Beatles are just a democratic group of middle-aged teenagers. We just don't happen to agree on doing concert tours. I've wanted to do some for a while [though not, McCartney could have added, when he'd suggested it], but I'm not sure anymore."

The possibility of playing live concerts was intriguing, but after the debacle at Twickenham, it would hardly have affected the Beatles' recording plans. Nothing could have persuaded them to undergo another bout of rehearsals under the pressure of creating new material. But another project under discussion in the spring of 1969 was sufficiently novel to rekindle their enthusiasm for work.

Back in 1964, Brian Epstein had negotiated a three-film deal for the Beatles with United Artists, both sides greeting the remarkable success of *A Hard Day's Night* as proof that there was little risk in a longer-term contract. *Help!* duly emerged in the summer of 1965, but thereafter the group's recording commitments forestalled work on another movie. In one of his last negotiations on their behalf, Epstein succeeded in selling UA the concept of a Beatle-related cartoon, for which his boys would supply the voices (eventually provided by actors) and the soundtrack (four songs, to be exact, fleshed out by material from their recent albums).

But even after *Yellow Submarine,* the Beatles owed UA a feature film, and in the spring of 1969 no one supposed that the documentary about their failure to stage a live show or finish an album could be it. There was no shortage of scripts on offer: the quartet had come close to agreeing on a Western called *A Talent for Loving* in 1965, and Epstein had commissioned a scurrilous, wickedly barbed satire *(Up against It)* from Joe Orton in 1967.

Orton's script was unfilmable, at least by the Beatles. Instead, after Epstein's death that summer, McCartney conceived the flawed project that became *Magical Mystery Tour.* The resounding denunciation of that stoned, whimsical exercise convinced the Beatles that any future film project would have to be founded on something altogether more secure— indeed, something as conservative as a script and a professional director.

Tired of portraying themselves on screen, whether au naturel (as in *A Hard Day's Night* and *Magical Mystery Tour*) or in cartoon form *(Help!),* the Beatles demanded roles in which they could lose their public identities. Early in 1968, they were sent an ambitious script for an adaptation of a fictional trilogy that had captured the spirit of the age: J. R. R. Tolkien's *The Lord of the Rings.* With its blend of myth, fantasy, and archetypal human conflicts, Tolkien's books had tantalized and delighted everyone from scholars of Icelandic sagas to schoolchildren, before reaching a new audience in the hippies of the late '60s.

Contractual problems over the film rights to the books sabotaged any chance of the Beatles' beginning work on *The Lord of the Rings* in 1968, but by the following spring the barriers had been removed. "All four Beatles have read the books," revealed Derek Taylor, "and they are very enthusiastic. After this idea, nothing else seems up to standard."

George Harrison was vocal in his support for the project. "It will be at least as big as *2001: A Space Odyssey* visually," he boasted to *Disc,* "with full stereo sound and cinerama. The story is fantastic, and we've agreed to let each other do exactly what we want to do with it." Harrison's optimism hinged on a new group philosophy, which he explained at length that spring: "We've got to a point where we can see each other quite clearly. And by allowing each other to be each other, we can become the Beatles again."

It was a misty-eyed vision of togetherness, though Lennon's hard-edged realism seemed unlikely to achieve total oneness with Harrison's vague spirituality: "I'm life, really, spiritually and mystically. And life is either up or down, in or out, left or right. Life is like the waves on the ocean. We're all like little boats on the surface of life. Some people are securely anchored. Now, as each day goes by, I feel myself becoming more and more securely anchored. The real me is the real you and the real him." Or "I am he and you are he and you are me and we are all together," as John Lennon had written eighteen months earlier. Then as spring passed into summer, the circle reopened, never to be closed again.

There's a standard version of the transition from the agonies of the *Get Back/Let It Be* album into the lush creativity of *Abbey Road.* In the eyes of producer George Martin, "*Let It Be* was a miserable experience, and I never thought that we would get back together again. So I was very surprised when Paul rang me up and said, 'We want to make another record. Will you produce it for us, really produce it?' I said, 'Yes, if I am really allowed to produce it. If I have to go back and accept a lot of instructions which I don't like, I won't do it.'" (*Melody Maker.*)

In reality, the border between *Get Back* and *Abbey Road* wasn't quite so precise. The latter was launched back in February 1969, with the initial work on Lennon's "I Want You (She's So Heavy)," but at this stage, the song was intended to help fill out *Get Back*. Even in April, Lennon was still unsure of the division of spoils between the soundtrack album and what might follow. Sessions continued into early May, without a clear target in sight.

The delivery of Glyn Johns's "final" edition of *Get Back, Don't Let Me Down, and Twelve Other Songs* provided a stark reminder of the group's past misdemeanors. "It's like an unfinished rehearsal for the show that we never did," Lennon commented bravely to the *New Musical Express* after hearing the acetate. "There's bits of dialogue on it, and 'Get Back' is the most finished tune, so you can imagine what some of it is like! But there are obviously some McCartney hits there, and there's one beautiful ballad called 'Let It Be' which is a cert for somebody, a cert." Lennon was realistic enough to know that his own contributions to *Get Back* scarcely fell into the "cert" category.

Speaking from his bed in Toronto, where the Lennons' second bed-in for peace was under way, John revealed to the *New Musical Express* that the group had already elected to abandon their audio vérité approach for their next record: "It will probably please the critics a bit more, because we got a bit tired of just sort of strumming along forever. We got a bit into production again. It's really something. So tell the armchair critics to hold their tongues and wait."

The evidence for his "really something" was still sparse: unfinished versions of "Something," "I Want You (She's So Heavy)," "Octopus's Garden," and "Oh! Darling," to be precise. But a return to the multitracking and tape editing that had been a trademark of their studio work through 1967 and 1968 represented an abrupt change of direction from the January 1969 sessions.

Through June 1969, the Beatles were on vacation, allowing McCartney—and, briefly, Lennon—to amass some new material. In seclusion in Surrey, John and Yoko celebrated Yoko's second pregnancy, due to reach full term in February 1970. Now mercifully clear of the heroin habit that had shadowed their activities since the previous winter, they schemed for peace and understanding, and cemented their indissoluble union as "Johnandyoko." Freed from obligations to the Beatles and to their lawyers, they enjoyed a brief respite from the public and media aggression they had endured for the previous year.

McCartney spent most of June in the United States with his Eastman in-laws, mulling over the consequences of his refusal to sign a management contract with Allen Klein. For the moment, though, he seemed to have been able to separate his battle with Klein from his relationship with the remaining Beatles. Since Harrison had now reached a state of universal beneficence, and Starr would go along with anything that didn't result in conflict, the Beatles' sessions scheduled to begin at the start of July should have been their most relaxed in years.

Eager for the fun to begin, McCartney arrived at EMI's Abbey Road studios early on the afternoon of 1 July, a day before the others were booked to arrive. While McCartney overdubbed a lead vocal onto "You Never Give Me Your Money," shifting without effort from the plaintive to the playful, Lennon was close to writing a premature end to the Beatles' story.

With Yoko and the couple's children, Julian Lennon and Kyoko Cox, Lennon was visiting the northernmost branches of his family in Scotland. An erratic driver at the best of times, he lost concentration for a few seconds and plowed the family's car off the road near Golspie. All four occupants were injured, Lennon and the children suffering cuts and bruises, the pregnant Ono crushing several vertebrae in her spine and receiving a severe enough blow on the head to cause a concussion. Instead of returning to London that night, the family was hospitalized in Scotland for five days.

The delay proved to be crucial. Harrison and Starr joined McCartney at Abbey Road on 2 July and blithely continued work on their album as if Lennon's input were scarcely required. Over the next week, the trio recorded McCartney's medley of "Golden Slumbers" and "Carry That Weight," plus Harrison's charmingly melodic "Here Comes the Sun." McCartney also nailed "Her Majesty," without bothering to add to the bare fragment of the song he'd unveiled in January.

On 9 July, the Lennons traipsed reluctantly into the studio from Surrey, where they had been convalescing since their return from Scotland. As engineer Phil McDonald told Mark Lewisohn, "We were all waiting for them to arrive, Paul, George and Ringo downstairs and us upstairs. They didn't know what state he would be in. There was a definite 'vibe': they were almost afraid of Lennon before he arrived, because they didn't know what he would be like. I got the feeling that the three of them were a little bit scared of him. When he did come in it was a relief, and they got together fairly well. John was a powerful figure, especially with Yoko—a double strength" *(The Complete Beatles Recording Sessions).*

Resigned to dealing with "Johnandyoko" as an indivisible entity, either half of which might act as spokesperson, the other Beatles were set further on edge by the peculiar circumstances under which the next few sessions would take place. If it was unsettling to attempt honest communication with Lennon while his partner and sometime collaborator sat silently alongside him, it was all the more unnerving when Yoko was delivered to the sessions by ambulance, on a stretcher, strapped into a brace. A bed was set up alongside Lennon's chair, a microphone lowered above her head, and Yoko remained a prone, but by no means neutral, observer of what ensued.

Lennon's very appearance illustrated some kind of commitment to the Beatles' collective project, although it's doubtful that he would have chosen to rejoin the fray had he realized what was on the agenda. To welcome back his increasingly distant colleague, McCartney elected to resume work on a song that had already consumed many unprofitable hours in January: "Maxwell's Silver Hammer." "That was so fruity," George Harrison complained after the sessions were over. "After a while, we did a good job on it, but when Paul got an idea or an arrangement in his head . . ." and his voice tailed off into tired disbelief. Lennon was equally dismissive to *Melody Maker,* though more oblique: "All I can say about 'Maxwell's Hammer,'" he sniped later that year, "is that I dig Engelbert Humperdinck as much as I dig John Cage, and I don't listen to either of them." The McCartney/Humperdinck comparison preyed on McCartney's mind.

While McCartney and to a lesser extent Starr were wholehearted in their commitment to the new album, Lennon and Harrison registered their psychological absence in diverse ways. Using Yoko's injuries as a convenient excuse, Lennon skipped several sessions over the ensuing weeks. His truancy almost certainly stemmed from the couple's renewed use of heroin, triggered by their car crash, but it was also due as much to what

they perceived, with some justification, as the hostility with which they were commonly regarded in Britain—and within the Beatles' own business empire. During the final week of August, Lennon completed work on "Cold Turkey," a brutally realistic account of the experience of sudden withdrawal from regular heroin use. "Thirty-six hours, rolling in pain . . . I'd promise you anything, get me out of this hell," he wrote—scarcely the perfect backdrop for adding anything constructive to "Here Comes the Sun," let alone "Maxwell's Silver Hammer."

Whatever the medical circumstances, it's noticeable that Lennon's absence often coincided with the times when less important songs—that is, Harrison's—were due to be recorded. He was missing when work continued on "Here Comes the Sun" and "Something"; he skipped the vocal harmony session for McCartney's "Oh! Darling." In fact, having officially returned to the group on 9 July, he made only the most token contributions

THE ALBUMS

to the next twelve days of sessions. But from 21 July onward, he was finally able to offer some new material of his own. Thereafter he was present at Abbey Road more often than not—which suggests that embarrassment at his own lack of creativity had also been a factor in his attendance record.

True to his role as the youngest member of the class, Harrison clocked in dutifully for every session, whether it was one of his songs or something "fruity" from McCartney that was due for consideration. But, as he revealed later to *Crawdaddy,* he found his own way of distancing himself from the group's inner tension:

> I used to have an experience when I was a kid which used to frighten me. I realised in meditation that I had the same experience, and it's something to do with always feeling really tiny. There was always this thing which I later related to the mantra, and this feeling would just go with it. I'd feel really tiny and at the same time I'd feel I was a whole thing as well. It was feeling like two different things at the same time.
>
> And this little thing, with this feeling that would vibrate right through me, would start off like rolling around and it would start getting bigger and bigger and faster and faster and faster, until it was going like so far and getting so fast that it was mind-boggling and I'd come out of it really scared.
>
> I used to get that experience when we were recording *Abbey Road.* I'd go into this big empty studio and get into a soundbox inside of it and do my meditation inside of there, and I had a couple of indications of that same experience, which I realised was the same one I had when I was a kid.

Through power play, role play, and the exchange of insecurities and resentments, the Beatles gradually assembled *Abbey Road.* "To me, listening to *Abbey Road* is like listening to somebody else," Harrison confided to *Disc* when the album was completed. "It doesn't feel like the Beatles." Maybe that was because the Beatles hadn't felt much like the Beatles when they were making it.

As the album took shape, George Martin and Paul McCartney assembled the medley—or, to be exact, the sequence of medleys—that would dominate the record's second side. This dazzling public display of unity, which is how it was viewed as the album was released, was accompanied by a series of symbolic get-togethers in August 1969.

The Beatles had always struggled to find suitable titles for their albums; in recent times, only *Sgt. Pepper* and the *Yellow Submarine* soundtrack had emerged naturally. *Rubber Soul* was a private joke, whereas *Revolver* had passed through a series of changes (*Abracadabra!* was the leading contender at one point). *The Beatles* was to be called *A Doll's House* until the British rock group Family nabbed the title from under their nose.

Engineer Geoff Emerick recalled that this final Beatles studio project was originally to be named *Everest* after the brand of cigarettes he smoked. Only when it was suggested that the group fly to the Himalayas for a cover shoot did a Beatle suggest that they could call the record *Abbey Road* and take the photo outside the studio. So it was that an album actually begun at two independent London locations, Trident Studios and Olympic Studios, was named after EMI's north London flagship.

On 8 August, photographer Iain Macmillan shot a reel of pictures as the four Beatles strolled back and forth across the pedestrian crossing outside the Abbey Road studios. In keeping with his creative domination of the group in their final year, this was a Paul McCartney concept, sketched in matchstick-man form during an earlier session. While Harrison wore the blue denim uniform of the American rock establishment, the others kept faith with Brian Epstein's early instructions and donned suits: Lennon, the brilliant white he'd adopted in his bid for peacenik sainthood; Ringo, young executive's black; McCartney, the casual blue-gray of a working-class hero enjoying a night on the town. It was the height of summer, and as the session progressed, McCartney took off his sandals and strolled barefoot across the striped tarmac.

Ten days later, the four Beatles began work on the stereo mixing and editing of *Abbey Road*. On 20 August, the four men were together in a recording studio for the last time. The following day, a stormy annual general meeting at Apple's West End headquarters acted as a reminder that their business relations had become intolerably strained. On 22 August, Lennon, McCartney, Harrison, and Starr posed for photographs—and a few minutes of silent film footage—at the Lennons' new home, Tittenhurst Park in Surrey (a session that produced the cover for the 1970 LP *Hey Jude*). Weighed down by facial hair and the knowledge that their decade-long unity was now largely a facade, they stared impassively at the camera lens. When the session was over, so effectively were the Beatles.

In public, the Beatles appeared to be working in complete harmony during August and September 1969. Although the progress of the *Get Back* project was still uncertain—Apple was now saying it would be delayed for another couple of months—the news that the group had since completed another album was widely regarded as proof that their internal feuds had abated.

With his usual devotion to the cause, Apple press officer Derek Taylor announced eagerly that "the [new] album is very compact and very real, and was recorded at nice, workmanlike sessions which usually began at 2 P.M. and continued until the end of the evening." Apple also let slip that "most of the songs have been written by Paul McCartney," and Taylor boasted that "Paul has had to stop writing for a while because of a tremendous backlog of material which is building up."

For his own part, McCartney enthused that the second side's medley "lasts as long as it takes to have a bath, get out, dry yourself and get dressed," while Starr added, "The second side is incredible. I like the boys playing together, you know. I like [being in] a group."

Even Harrison subsumed his individual needs beneath the corporate message: "I believe that if I'm going to sing songs on record, they might as well be my own. I feel that I can say more in two minutes of a song than in ten years [of talking]. But I don't want the Beatles to be recording rubbish for my sake, just because I wrote it. And on the other hand, I don't want to record rubbish, just because they wrote it. The group comes first."

But in the same *Disc* interview, designed to plug *Abbey Road* as a statement of Beatles togetherness, Harrison let slip a chink of realism: "With the Beatles, it's sometimes a matter of whoever pushes hardest gets the most tunes on the album. Then it's down to personalities as to whoever's going to push. And more often, I just leave it until somebody would like to do one of my tunes."

Of all the Beatles, it was Lennon who had consistently shown the least interest in Harrison's tunes over the years. Now, behind the scenes, he began to maneuver for freedom not only from supporting Harrison but from McCartney as well. Two weeks before *Abbey Road* was released, Lennon visited Abbey Road and demanded the tapes for a Beatles recording left unfinished after sessions in both 1967 and 1968 of his own song "What's the New Mary Jane." In truth, the track featured only one other Beatle—ironically enough, Harrison—but it had still been under consideration for *The Beatles* right up to the final forty-eight-hour mixing session in October 1968.

Lennon's hijacking of the tapes, which no one at Abbey Road would have dreamed of questioning, actually had a sinister purpose. With a symbolism that is only too apparent in retrospect, he was taking what was ostensibly a Beatles song and planning to release it as a single by his own Plastic Ono Band, the conceptual unit he'd "formed" that summer as a vehicle for his antiwar anthem, "Give Peace a Chance."

That same day, 11 September, Lennon informed Allen Klein, manager for three of the group, that he was quitting the Beatles. The next morning, he was invited to take part in a rock 'n' roll revival festival being held that weekend in Toronto. He rounded up an impromptu Plastic Ono Band lineup, featuring Klaus Voormann, Eric Clapton, Alan White, Yoko Ono, but (pointedly) no other Beatles; flew across the Atlantic; and performed at Toronto's Varsity Stadium in front of thirty thousand initially ecstatic, then—as Yoko followed half a dozen Lennon rock oldies with an avant-garde screamfest—bewildered spectators.

"I knew I was leaving before we went to Toronto," Lennon said later. "I told Eric and Klaus that I was leaving, and that I'd probably like to use them as a group." Eight months after he'd suggested replacing George Harrison with Clapton, Lennon was prepared to ditch all of the Beatles and start afresh.

Abbey Road was officially released on 26 September 1969. Earlier that week, Lennon and McCartney endured one final round of business discussions and arguments—John trumpeting the increased royalty rate that Allen Klein had squeezed out of EMI and Capitol, Paul emphasizing that he could never accept Klein as his manager, and that he had instructed his brother-in-law, John Eastman, to inform all the Beatles' legal partners and opponents of that fact.

Lennon had one final card to play: he told McCartney, and possibly the other Beatles as well, that he wanted them to record "Cold Turkey" as the group's next single, for immediate release. When Paul understandably demurred—of all Lennon's songs to date, "Cold Turkey" was a personal statement, not a collective one—John used this as a pretext for quitting

George tries his hand at the drums.

COURTESY OF PHOTOFEST

the group. "I'm leaving," he told the stunned McCartney. "I want a divorce."

Aware that the announcement of a split might cripple the promotional campaign for *Abbey Road,* and hopeful that Lennon's declaration might prove to be mere bluster, both Klein and McCartney suggested that John could do what he liked, but he should keep his decision private until the group made a collective decision about their future. Lennon concurred. It was a rare misjudgment from a man who showed a naive, but genuine, talent for publicity: concealing his decision allowed McCartney to seize the initiative the following spring and announce his own departure from the Beatles the same week that his first solo album was released. Even in his anger Lennon couldn't help but be impressed by his ex-partner's canny abilities as a PR man.

LET IT BE / ABBEY ROAD

Abbey Road appeared without incident or argument at the end of September, to generally ecstatic reviews, and the carefully leaked whisper that McCartney, Starr, and George Martin all considered it to be the Beatles' best album to date. Depending on one's criteria, it remains a defensible position. *Abbey Road* mirrored the stylistic range of *The White Album,* but eliminated what George Martin had viewed as the self-indulgence. There was no "Revolution 9" on *Abbey Road,* for instance, no "Wild Honey Pie" or "Why Don't We Do It in the Road." Instead, the album was an almost miraculous parade of commercial pop songs, with a melodic flow and invention rarely matched in the group's catalog. In particular, the much vaunted second-side medley, the long construction of song fragments from "You Never Give Me Your Money" to "The End," demonstrated that no one could string together aural entertainment with the same verve and skill as Paul McCartney. Despite Lennon's contributions, the medley sounds like a dry run for all of McCartney's solo work in the '70s—although only on 1971's *Ram* did he ever come close to matching it.

This wasn't the Beatles' image that John Lennon wanted to choose and preserve, and for all its brilliant gloss, *Abbey Road* was lacking in subtexts. It didn't pretend to be anything other than the ultimate pop record. And by 1969, Lennon was tired of pop.

The opposing views of McCartney and Lennon were reflected by the album's structure, at least in its original vinyl form. Side 1 was devoted to distinctly separate tracks, linked by nothing more concrete than Beatles professionalism. Side 2 was dominated by short cycles of songs, or song fragments. As Lennon noted cynically, "they weren't real songs, they were just bits and pieces stuck together."

Much of side 2 may indeed have been inconsequential, but never has fluff been so superbly packaged. From start to finish, the sequence is a triumph of commercial record-making, a dazzling cornucopia of killer hooks and effortless ear candy. Stuffed to the brim with ideas, gimmicks, and finesse, it boasts the group's finest musicianship on record, some of the most sublime vocal harmonies ever captured on tape, and enough joyful craftsmanship to last most other groups a lifetime.

What was missing, as Lennon would have been the first to register, was emotional commitment, and any sense that a pop record was more than a delicious form of entertainment. To his ears, the bare, imageless lyrics of "I Want You (She's So Heavy)" said more than a thousand medleys. For Lennon, a record was now a confessional. For McCartney, it was a kaleidoscopic theater for the senses. For the last time, in the summer of 1969, the Beatles' name was big enough to contain both extremes.

In the past, every shift in the group's image and sound had quickly been echoed by the rest of the pop world. But *Abbey Road* was such a perfect encapsulation of '60s pop that virtually no one else chose to imitate it. Nineteen seventy did not bring a flurry of albums dominated by carefully constructed medleys. The ultimate pop confection, *Abbey Road* could only be parodied, not emulated. Too contrived for the rock underground to copy, too complex for the bubblegum pop brigade to follow, the album influenced no one—except its main creator, Paul McCartney, who wasted years trying to recreate its effortless brilliance.

To the public, unaware of the angst that had been a constant backdrop since January, *Abbey Road* was simply further proof of the Beatles' pop genius. The album was greeted with almost universal praise, and it sold as quickly and as extensively as anything that had preceded it. Allen Klein broke one of the first rules for U.K. Beatle releases by waiting until the LP was in the shops and then selecting two of its songs, Harrison's "Something" and Lennon's "Come Together," as a double A-sided single. Previously, no Beatles single in Britain had been pulled from an album that was already on sale. "Something" was George's first A-side, and his song rapidly became established as a classic—further improving the already remarkable sales figures.

There was, however, an ironic postscript to the album's release. Having carefully maintained the facade of group unity while the record was promoted, McCartney then found himself the target of a bizarre U.S. media campaign, which claimed that he was dead, that he had been replaced in the Beatles by an impostor at the end of 1966, and that the group's subsequent records—and, more important, their packaging— were replete with "clues" confirming the tragedy. Most of these clues were said to be hidden on earlier albums, from *Sgt. Pepper* (McCartney faces away from the camera on the back cover) through *The Beatles* ("Paul is dead," Lennon is supposed to whisper after "I'm So Tired," "miss him, miss him"). But the *Abbey Road* cover provided the rumormongers with the most damning evidence of a conspiracy. Paul has bare feet (i.e., he's dead); he's out of step with the others (i.e., he's definitely dead); and there's a car in the frame with a mysterious license plate (28IF), denoting that McCartney would have been twenty-eight if he'd lived (he'd have been twenty-seven, actually, but what was a year among corpses?).

The currency this fanciful tale achieved in the United States, and then around the world, suggested that the Beatles and their public image were so closely entwined by the end of the '60s that the imminent disintegration of the group had insidiously filtered into the collective unconscious. Unable to deal with the idea that any one of the Beatles might want to destroy the "all-for-one, one-for-all" myth, a generation of fans convinced themselves that the destruction had been engineered from without—that one of the legendary quartet had been stolen away by cruel fate, and that the remaining trio's brave attempt to disguise their loss was now beginning to crack.

One bizarre result of the "Paul Is Dead" cult was that it diverted attention from the Beatles' real plight: the fight to maintain the group as a working unit. So concerned was the media with the suggestion that McCartney was dead that they missed the very real possibility that it wasn't Paul who had been killed, but the unity known as the Beatles. Stranger still is the fact that no one who was party to Lennon's decision, even John himself, made the slightest public reference to his unequivocal break from the group. Instead, the two most disaffected Beatles, John and George, continued to give regular interviews through the final weeks of 1969, purely to promote the group's recent releases.

Harrison was prepared to admit to the *New Musical Express* that "it took time for me to get more confidence as a songwriter, and now I don't care if the others don't like my songs. I can shrug it off." But at the same time, he was happy to look beyond *Abbey Road* to another Beatles album—and he wasn't talking about *Get Back,* still stuck in limbo after almost a year—where "we're going to get an equal rights thing so we'll all have as much as each other on the album." At the same time, he conceded that "I've also thought of doing an album of my own, mainly just to get rid of all the songs I've got stacked up. At the rate of two or three on each Beatles album, I'm not even going to get the ones I've [already] done out for three or four years." But in a climate where Lennon could issue Plastic Ono Band singles alongside Beatles records, and where he had

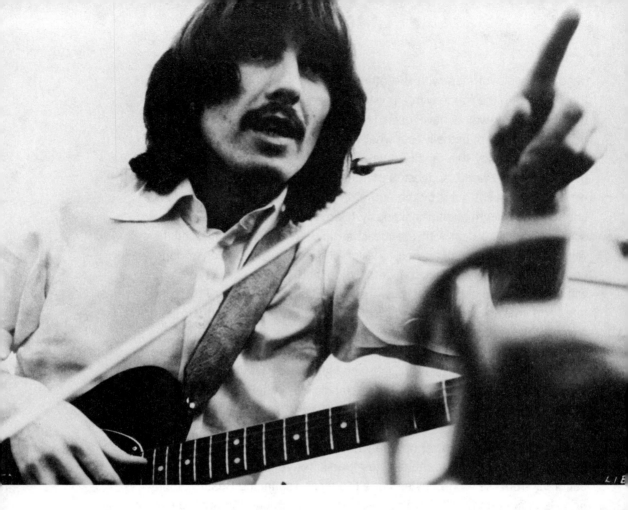

Harrison at work.
Courtesy of Photofest

openly encouraged George to make a solo record of his own, Harrison's individual projects needed not threaten the collective future.

Lennon publicly agreed in the *New Musical Express:* "George has got songs he's been trying to get on our records since 1920. He's got to make an album of his own. Maybe if he puts 'Beatles' on the label rather than 'George Harrison,' it might sell more. That's the drag." But John was also forthright about the fact that the word "Beatles" didn't mean the same thing that it had in 1964: "My 'Cold Turkey' has got Ringo and me on, and yet half the Beatles' tracks on *Abbey Road,* I'm not on. Or half the tracks on the double album—and even way back. Sometimes there might be only two Beatles on a track. It's got to the situation where if we have the name 'Beatle' on it, it sells. So you start to think: what are we selling? Do they buy it because it's worth it, or just because it says Beatles?"

Alone of the quartet, Lennon was willing to philosophize that autumn about their collective future. "The Beatles can go on appealing to a wide audience as long as they make albums like *Abbey Road*," he mused in *Melody Maker,* adding with an air of malice, "which have nice little folk-songs like 'Maxwell's Silver Hammer' for the grannies to dig." On a personal level, he revealed that "Paul and I both have differences of opinion on how things should be run. But instead of it being a private argument about how an LP should be done, or a certain track, it's now a larger argument about the organisation of Apple itself. Whether we both want the same thing from Apple is a matter of opinion. But where we [really] digress is how to achieve it.

"There's also a problem with the four of us holding different opinions, and the Apple staff not knowing where they are or who to listen to. The result is that we kept sending in different instructions, and nothing was being done. Like people anywhere, they were getting away with what they could. What I want is for the freeloading to stop, but the old Apple spirit to remain." On this, at least, Lennon and McCartney were in agreement.

One *New Musical Express* journalist dared to give voice to the secret fear that haunted Beatledom: would the group split up? Lennon was non-committal: "It depends how much we want to record together. I don't know if we want to do it again. I go off and on it, I really do. The problem is that in the old days, when we needed an album, Paul and I got together and produced enough songs for it. Nowadays there's three of us writing prolifically and trying to fit it all onto one album. I don't want to spend six months making an album I have two tracks on, and neither do Paul or George. If we can overcome that, maybe it'll sort itself out. We didn't spend ten years making it, getting the freedom to use the recording studio, to be background musicians."

With his laconic acceptance of the status quo, Lennon briefly approached a public realization of the inevitable: "It's nothing new, the way things are. It's just human. We've always said we've had fights. It's no news that we argue." The real news was that, by the final weeks of 1969, Lennon and McCartney had passed beyond argument; Lennon could discuss the Beatles' future with a journalist, but not with the man who'd been his artistic collaborator for more than a decade.

The void that succeeded the release of *Abbey Road* should have been filled by the imminent arrival of the *Get Back* album and movie. Postponed while the new studio record was whisked through the system, the project was rescheduled for September 1969, then November, then bumped into the New Year. In October, the situation was complicated when American radio stations obtained a tape copy of the version of the album Glyn Johns had prepared in late March—which the Beatles had collectively rejected, though they couldn't quite bring themselves to scrap the project.

When *Rolling Stone* and then *New Musical Express* carried reviews of the Johns tape, and the new underground bootleg industry produced its own version of *Get Back,* cunningly retitled *Kum Back,* Apple and the Beatles realized that the project had to be brought to some kind of resolution. As late as October 1969, there was still talk that there would be two *Get Back* films: two hours for TV, three for cinema presentation. But the continual indecision left the project's creators, notably director Michael Lindsay-Hogg, frustrated. By the end of 1969, he'd submitted an eighty-eight-minute cut of the movie, now provisionally retitled *Let It Be,* presumably on the basis that McCartney's elegiac ballad could be retrieved from the soundtrack as a tie-in single.

Both Lennon and McCartney were working in the studio during November 1969, and Apple suggested coyly that they were contributing to the film project. In fact, Lennon was revamping not one but two Beatles leftovers for a solo single ("You Know My Name [Look up the Number]" had also miraculously switched allegiance). Only McCartney's pained intervention prevented the release of "What's the New Mary Jane" as a Plastic Ono Band 45.

Meanwhile, Paul was working on certain undefined "tracks," which would prove to be the seeds for his first solo album. But when it became obvious that *Get Back, Let It Be,* or whatever was finally going to be released as a movie, McCartney shouldered the obligation of completing a suitable tie-in Beatles record.

Lindsay-Hogg's footage included ragged performances of two songs that hadn't appeared on Glyn Johns's *Get Back* LP: Lennon's "Across the Universe" and Harrison's "I Me Mine." Neither had been performed to anything like the Beatles' usual professional standards during the making of the film. "Across the Universe" did exist in earlier form, having been taped by the Beatles in February 1968 for use on a charity album (which eventually appeared in December 1969). But if the Beatles needed a take of "I Me Mine" for the soundtrack album, they'd have to record one.

McCartney, Harrison, and Starr went through the motions of alerting Lennon that they'd booked a studio for 3–4 January 1970 and that his presence would be appreciated. Instead, John and Yoko left England just before New Year for Denmark, where they cut their hair, discussed a forthcoming peace festival, and enthusiastically agreed to finance a flying machine that could run without fuel.

Back in London, the three remaining Beatles were in a less idealistic mood, though Harrison could still raise a smile. Referring to the recent split of a late '60s British pop band, he quipped before take 15 of "I Me Mine": "You all will have read that Dave Dee is no longer with us. But Micky and Tich and I would just like to carry on the good work that's always gone down in [EMI studio] No. 2." Almost exactly a year after McCartney, Harrison, and Starr had performed "I Me Mine" at Twickenham, the trio assembled a ninety-four-second version of the song, throwing together guitar, keyboard, and vocal overdubs in ten professional, productive hours.

The following day, the three Beatles and producer George Martin gathered again—to add backing vocals to McCartney's "Let It Be," for Harrison to overdub a new guitar solo alongside the one he'd added in April, and for the group to supervise the addition of brass and strings to the track. On 5 January, Glyn Johns completed the mixing of "I Me Mine," and hurriedly added that song, the revised "Let It Be," and "Across the Universe" to the lineup of the soundtrack LP. One song, McCartney's "Teddy Boy," was dropped from the original running order, because Paul had already rerecorded it for his solo record—this time without sarcastic interjections from Lennon.

For the second time, a *Get Back* LP was finished. Copies were duly forwarded to all four Beatles. McCartney's attitude seems to have been "grimace and bear it"; Harrison and Starr concurred that, in Ringo's words, "the album needed fixing." But Lennon regarded *Get Back* as "the shittiest load of badly recorded shit with a lousy feeling to it ever." And without his approval, there could be no album—and no film.

On 27 January 1970, John Lennon wrote "Instant Karma!" around the same chord sequence he'd utilized for "All You Need Is Love." That evening, he recorded the song with the Plastic Ono Band: Klaus Voormann and Alan White, plus George Harrison. Producing the session was Phil Spector, in town at the invitation of Allen Klein.

The most celebrated and controversial record producer of the '60s, famed for his "wall of sound" technique and feared for his obsessive, tempestuous personality, Spector had known the Beatles since 1964. He'd accompanied the group on their first flight to the United States, and all four Beatles had been vocal in their enthusiasm for his work. "If we ever used anybody besides George Martin," Lennon enthused in 1965, "it would [have to] be Spector."

By January 1970, Spector was widely believed to have passed his prime, and he needed the kudos of a superstar rock artist—a Dylan, a Stone, or a Beatle—to reestablish his reputation in the ultrafickle American music industry. Though Spector was suspicious, sometimes publicly, of Klein's reputation, he was also aware that the manager held the entrance key to the Beatles' chaotic empire. Early in 1970, the pair came to an arrangement whereby Phil would "accidentally" happen to be in London when Lennon next needed a producer—which, at his current work rate, was likely to be sooner rather than later. Spector duly passed his audition with "Instant Karma!" Instead of the tinny, stodgy sound Lennon had achieved as artist-producer on "Cold Turkey," Spector built "Karma!" into a light but gutsy piece of rock-soul, hinged around percussive pianos and a street choir of partygoers plucked from a London nightclub.

Flushed with enthusiasm, Lennon invited Spector to survey the *Get Back* tapes. In the absence of a definite veto, United Artists Films had tentatively scheduled the release of the *Let It Be* movie—the title was now definite—for May 1970. EMI and Apple prepared for the release of the title song as a single in March, with the LP to follow in April.

Lennon requested Spector's assistance in February, but—as Ringo Starr explained in *Melody Maker*—"it was a strange time for us then, because we weren't doing anything, but he couldn't fix the album unless we said so. So we all said yes." "If you want to work with us, go and do your audition," Lennon told the mercurial producer. But he didn't begin work until 23 March, presumably because he was waiting for approval from all the other Beatles. One doesn't need a private investigator to imagine who held out longest, though as Ringo noted, "Even Paul said yes at the beginning."

John enjoying playing again on the roof.
COURTESY OF PHOTOFEST

On 8 March, "Let It Be" was issued as the Beatles' final British single, backed by the hastily retrieved tapes of "You Know My Name (Look up the Number)"—Lennon now agreed that it was a Fab Four track after all. That week, Lennon and Ono entered a long period of primal therapy with Dr. Arthur Janov, first in London, then in the United States. This violent period of psychological excavation had one effect on the *Let It Be* project: it removed Lennon as an active force once and for all. In his absence, and with McCartney hard at work on his own solo album, it was left to Harrison and Starr to supervise Spector in the studio.

As the Beatles' official record producer—though he'd been absent from many sessions over the previous two years—George Martin felt some proprietary interest in the progress of the soundtrack LP. "I knew that John was going in the studios, doing some work on *Let It Be*," he said to *Melody Maker* in 1971, "but I understood that as they were making a film of it, they were doing some film tracks." Lennon wasn't anywhere near Abbey Road studios during Spector's brief stay, but another Beatle was— Paul McCartney, who was working on his solo album within the same building. As Spector set about "ruining" one of McCartney's favorite Beatles tracks, Paul himself seems to have been completely oblivious to the producer's presence. That's difficult to believe; more likely, McCartney was so estranged from Lennon and the *Let It Be* concept by March 1970 that he'd simply washed his hands of the whole affair, and preferred ignorance to confrontation. It's also likely that, used to producers and engineers who obeyed his instructions implicitly, he underestimated Spector's nerve.

As he later told *Rolling Stone,* Spector entered the project with few illusions: "It was no favor to me to give me George Martin's job, because I don't consider him in my league. He's an arranger, that's all. He had left the album in deplorable condition [though of course it was Glyn Johns who had prepared the *Get Back* LP], and it was not satisfactory to any of them. They did not want it out as it was. So John said, 'Let Phil do it,' and I said, 'Fine.' Then I said, 'Would anybody like to get involved in it, work on it with me?' 'No.' They didn't care."

Most producers would have been overawed by the responsibility of salvaging a Beatles album. Phil Spector approached it as just another exercise in artist manipulation. In the early '60s, he'd ruthlessly placed his own needs before those of the acts on his label; now, faced with another legend in disarray, he elected to remake the Beatles in his own image. Since he was nothing if not a remarkable auteur, his methods were both singular and dramatic. Reviewing the tapes left by Glyn Johns, he flung himself into the project with childlike enthusiasm and excess. But as ever, he proved himself as much a master of subtle retouching as of the grand gesture.

In nine days, he transformed Johns's *Get Back* from an audio vérité disaster into a strange hybrid of production extravaganza and threadbare documentary. At its most delicate, his artistry was sublime. He brought three-dimensional clarity to the flat acoustics of "Two of Us," invested "Dig a Pony" with real muscle, and refined the brittle rockabilly of "The One after 909" until it was razor sharp. The Band had already alerted the Beatles to the fact that other artists were achieving a visceral sound beyond the ken of George Martin. Spector proved that the right pair of hands could create that richness and depth at Abbey Road.

More controversially, Spector dared to tamper with the group's original concept for *Let It Be.* Glyn Johns had been instructed to convey the impression that these were spontaneous live performances. The American abandoned that manifesto on 1 April 1970, when he invited thirty-six musicians and fourteen singers to overdub lush, monstrous textures onto three songs: "Across the Universe," "I Me Mine," and, most controversially, "The Long and Winding Road." Over the Beatles' erratic performance of McCartney's ballad was layered a froth of heavenly voices and singing strings. Spector believed he was simply responding to the song's natural sentimentality. McCartney was too stunned to know what to think.

When Spector had finished work, the Beatles received their third set of acetates for the star-crossed film soundtrack. Lennon's reaction was relief: "I didn't puke. He made something of it. He did a great job. After months of this black cloud hanging over me, this was going to go out." In *Melody Maker,* Ringo Starr remembered McCartney's response: "He heard it. I spoke to him on the phone and said, 'Did you like it?' and he said, 'Yeah, it's okay.' He didn't put it down. And then suddenly he didn't want it to go out . . . two weeks after that, he wanted to cancel it."

A lot happened in those two weeks. McCartney had completed work on his first solo album, and he demanded that it be released immediately—in mid-April, just before *Let It Be* was scheduled to reach the stores. As directors of Apple Records, Lennon, Harrison, and Starr requested that he delay his album and let the Beatles' record appear first. Armed with official letters stating their case, Starr visited McCartney at his London home: "I didn't think it fair that some office lad should take something like that round . . . so I said, 'Send it up, I'll take it round.' But he got angry, because we were asking him to hold his album back and the [*McCartney*] album was very important to him. He was stabbing his fingers at me, and saying, 'I'll get you! You'll pay for this!' He told me to get out of his house. He was crazy. He went crazy, I thought. I got very brought down, because I couldn't believe this was happening to me. I'm very emotional: things like that really upset me." (*Melody Maker.*)

Stunned by Paul's intransigence, Ringo told the others that if Paul's album was so important to him, maybe they should just let him have his way. *McCartney* was rush released, complete with a press pack that featured a coy, self-serving "promotional" interview. "Did you miss the other Beatles and George Martin?" Paul was asked. The answer was no. "Do you foresee a time when Lennon/McCartney becomes an active songwriting partnership again?" "No." "What do you feel about John's peace effort?" "It doesn't give me any pleasure." And in an aside that said much about McCartney's attitude toward his music in spring 1970, he was asked, "Were you pleased with *Abbey Road*?" "It was a good album," he replied, and then clarified what he meant: "[It was] No. 1 for a long time."

It was a remarkable piece of self-promotion at his colleagues' expense and a blatant manipulation of the media, impressing and angering Lennon at the same time. Instead of the Beatles' myth staggering on through the summer, fueled by a film and a "new" album, McCartney's PR interview evoked "Beatles Split" headlines around the world. Apple's Derek Taylor made one last attempt to bridge the chasm: "Ringo and John and George and Paul are alive and well and full of hope. The world is still spinning and so are we and so are you. When the spinning stops—that'll be the time to worry, not before. Until then, the Beatles are alive and well and the beat goes on, the beat goes on." But even this eternal optimist sounded unconvincing.

Let It Be, the album and film, finally emerged in May 1970—just sixteen months after the sessions at Twickenham Studios and Apple. Lennon "felt sick when I saw the movie"; McCartney had the same reaction when he listened again to the record. "Paul wrote to tell me that he was pretty appalled," George Martin said in *Melody Maker* the following year. "When the record came out, I got a hell of a shock. I knew nothing about it, and neither did Paul. All the lush, un-Beatle-like orchestrations with harps and choirs in the background—it was so contrary to what John asked for in the first place." Martin concluded with a sound bite he's repeated ever since: "I wanted the credit changed to 'Produced by George Martin, Over-Produced by Phil Spector.'" His fellow survivor of the Twickenham sessions, Glyn Johns, was even more disgusted: "Phil Spector overdubbed a lot of bullshit all over it, strings and choirs and yuck." (Not that Johns's judgment was altogether reliable: his summary of the January 1969 sessions in *The Record Producers* a decade later was that "the whole mood was wonderful . . . there was all this nonsense going on at the time about the problems surrounding the group . . . in fact, they were having a wonderful time and being incredibly funny. I didn't stop laughing for six weeks.")

McCartney and Martin were equally affronted by the sleeve note Allen Klein added to the back cover, which boasted that *Let It Be* was a "new phase Beatles album," with "the warmth and the freshness of a live performance, as reproduced for disc by Phil Spector."

Lennon remained unrepentant about his approval of the album but hated the film, bemoaning the fact that "the camerawork was set up to show Paul and not anybody else." Starr agreed: "Michael Lindsay-Hogg liked Paul, I would think, more than the rest of us. So it's like Paul's film, actually. It was supposed to be 25 percent each, and I've got about two shots. I did a lot of my comedy for them. I ran round hiding and peeping and looning about, but they never used any of it."

At the same time, Starr was less than enthusiastic about the LP: "I never play it." But he described the situation within the Beatles with optimism ("everything's fine"), while Harrison chimed in that "we've got unity through diversity. We still see each other, still make contact. But we had to find ourselves, individually, one day. It was the natural course of events. I'm trying to do my own album now, but after that I'm ready to go back with the others."

Rumors of a reunion were regularly revived by the media for the rest of 1970. In December, Lennon, Harrison, and McCartney met in New York and agreed to hold a full Beatles conference in London the following month. Apple confirmed that a reunion was in the air. But two of the protagonists were working on private agendas. The same week that Lennon and McCartney had made their peace in New York, Lennon gave a lengthy interview to *Rolling Stone* editor Jann Wenner. Published soon after Christmas, it shattered any hope of a rapprochement with its vicious attacks on the other Beatles, especially McCartney, and their attitude toward Yoko.

McCartney, meanwhile, returned to London—and then shocked the other three by serving them with legal papers, announcing his intention to seek an official dissolution of the Beatles' financial and business partnership in the High Court. The writs were duly processed on New Year's Eve, and the early months of 1971 brought a bitter courtroom battle, eventually won by McCartney, which revived several long-standing disputes and made public some of the more unsavory episodes in the group's recent history. Ahead lay an unseemly battle in song between Lennon and McCartney, and years of bickering that lasted until John was murdered in New York on 8 December 1980.

Strangely, even while the court battle was raging, the saga of *Get Back, Abbey Road,* and *Let It Be* produced two final twists. First, the

Beatles' collective mouthpiece, Apple Records, announced an unlikely spin-off from the *Get Back* sessions: an imminent album featuring versions of the Beatles' favorite rock oldies, rescued from the Twickenham and Apple sessions. The briefest exposure to the endless bootlegs of the sessions would reveal the emptiness of that promise. But as an exercise in shattering the Beatles myth, the *Rock and Roll* LP vainly promised by Apple could hardly have been bettered.

A few weeks later, the recipients of the annual Oscar awards were announced in Hollywood. Who was responsible for the best original movie score of the previous twelve months? The Beatles, with their critically panned *Let It Be* LP. And who collected the award on their behalf? Paul McCartney, the man who'd felt "sick" when he heard what Phil Spector had done to the album. A long and winding road, to be sure . . .

THE SONGS

LET IT BE

Two of Us
(John Lennon/Paul McCartney)
Recorded 31 January 1969

Whose song was "Two of Us"? "Mine," asserted John Lennon in a 1980 interview, and it has passed into Beatles legend as, at the very least, a final collaboration between Lennon and McCartney.

The session tapes tell another story. On 2 January 1969, the first day of the Twickenham sessions, Paul McCartney schooled the rest of the Beatles, Lennon included, through the basic structure of the song. It continued to develop over the following month, and there's no hint on the surviving tapes that Lennon was anything more than a semi-interested observer of the song's creation.

"Two of Us" was originally intended as an electric rock song, and two different arrangements were glimpsed briefly in the final cut of the *Let It Be* movie. The 2 January tapes illustrate the problems that McCartney found in linking the verses, eventually settling on a syncopated guitar riff that Lennon found difficult to master. The middle eight was another conundrum: though McCartney arrived at the sessions with the melody and lyrics intact, he originally wanted this section to be played at double the speed of the rest of the song, a transition the other Beatles repeatedly failed to make.

The group's initial progress on the song soon dissipated, and on 6 January "Two of Us" sparked a furious row between McCartney and

George Harrison, ostensibly over the guitar arrangement, although by that point their disagreement clearly required little fuel.

The *Let It Be* film included a short clip of an 8 January performance that proved to be the apogee of the electric arrangement. A day later, again as documented in the film, the song provoked another bout of bickering, this time between McCartney and Lennon. After Harrison's departure from the group on 10 January, the song was set aside for two weeks.

Even within the milder atmosphere at the Apple studio, however, "Two of Us" failed to settle into a comfortable groove. On 24 January, having complained that the arrangement was "very stiff," Lennon pinpointed the dilemma: "For the electric [guitar], we've got to think of something. The problem is always the same, and the answer is always the same." Engineer-producer Glyn Johns seized this opportunity to remind the group of a suggestion he'd made in the first days at Twickenham: "Two of Us" should be performed on acoustic guitars.

The acoustic arrangement fell together in minutes, McCartney centering the song around the simplest of guitar riffs. Glyn Johns selected the day's best attempt for his initial lineup of the *Get Back* album, while another rather sluggish take was exhumed for *Anthology 3.* But "Two of Us" was still in transition at this point. The next day, the song's bass riff was perfected by Harrison on his six-string acoustic, while McCartney continued to drive the Beatles through endless retakes until he was satisfied with the whistling he envisaged over the fade-out.

Finally, on 31 January, the group was filmed and taped delivering the definitive rendition of the song. The first two takes were considered too slow and out of tune, but two further run-throughs were more successful, and the first of them—officially take 11—surfaced on both the *Let It Be* LP and in the film.

Though Lennon trivialized the song during rehearsals, improvising a line about "smoking someone's hard-earned grass," the completed lyrics presented a touching, if idealized, vision of a romantic relationship. Their sweet nostalgia doubled as a valedictory portrait of the two songwriters' fading camaraderie: "You and I have memories, longer than the road that stretches out ahead."

Dig a Pony
(JOHN LENNON/PAUL MCCARTNEY)
RECORDED 30 JANUARY 1969

"Dig a Pony" was one of the song fragments that John Lennon brought to the first of the Twickenham sessions.

He demonstrated it to Harrison with "Don't Let Me Down" and "I've Got a Feeling" before the first rehearsals began, admitting that "every song's got the same chords." During the first week of the sessions, the Beatles made a halfhearted attempt to master the song, to no one's great enthusiasm. By 7 January, McCartney could only greet Lennon's reintroduction of "Dig a Pony" with a conspicuous yawn.

The song's lyrics were, as Lennon conceded, "interchangeable," and when serious rehearsals resumed at Apple on 22 January, he admitted that he was inspired less by the meaning of the words than by their sound: "Lots of d's and b's." When Harrison queried the order of the verses, Lennon admitted, "I just make it up as I go along," and he continued to do so even as the final version of the song was being taped on the Apple rooftop a week later.

Given the general level of musical competence in January 1969, it is perhaps surprising that the Beatles seem to have experienced little difficulty in mastering the unfamiliar waltz tempo of the introduction. On 22 January, McCartney suggested adding a falsetto repeat of the chorus line "All I want is you" as a finale. An early stab at the new arrangement was included on *Anthology 3*. A day later, they were ready for Glyn Johns to tape "complete" versions of the song, one of which appeared on the *Get Back* acetate. But the officially released version of "Dig a Pony" on the *Let It Be* LP was taken from the live performance on the Apple rooftop on 30 January, though Phil Spector discreetly edited the performance for the album, stripping away the half-line of lyrics that had led into the first verse.

Across the Universe
(JOHN LENNON/PAUL McCARTNEY)
RECORDED 4, 8 FEBRUARY 1968;
1 APRIL 1970

The only performance on *Let It Be* or *Abbey Road* to predate 1969, "Across the Universe" proved frustratingly elusive as far as its composer was concerned. "It was a lousy track of a great song," John Lennon commented to *Playboy* in 1980, "and I was so disappointed by it. The guitars are out of tune and I'm singing out of tune, because I'm philosophically destroyed and nobody's supporting me or helping me with it, and the song was never done properly."

Lennon's dismissal of the performance is unfair, and seems to have been colored by his experiences during the Twickenham sessions. "Across the Universe" was originally written in the winter of 1967–68. "I was lying next to my first wife in bed," John recalled, "and I was irritated. She must have been going on and on about something, and she'd gone to sleep, and I kept hearing these words over and over, like an endless stream. I went downstairs and it turned into sort of a cosmic song rather than an irritated song. It drove me out of bed. I didn't want to write it."

The 1980 Lennon recognized that it was "one of the best lyrics I've written—in fact, it could be the best."

For all its poetics, "Across the Universe" was also one of Lennon's most personal lyrics—though its subject was not his feelings but the workings of his unconscious. In a rich web of images, he caught the mysterious sensuality of the creative process, "possessing and caressing me." The words evoked fleeting moments of artistic power, almost too delicate to catch, as "they slither while they pass, they slip away" or, in another verse, "thoughts meander like a restless wind." The irony was that only intense creative focus could have captured that transience. It was a remarkable piece of writing.

In February 1968, the Beatles spent five days working on songs for a new single, which would tide them over while they devoted several months—or so they'd planned—to studying meditation with the Maharishi Mahesh Yogi in India. Paul McCartney donated "Lady Madonna" to the sessions; Harrison arrived with the already recorded backing track for his parade of spiritual homilies, "The Inner Light."

Lennon began to lead them through "Across the Universe" on 4 February, unable to recreate the song's miraculous inspiration in music. It was not for want of trying: Harrison picked out the introductory motif on sitar, and also provided a droning tamboura as the backdrop, while Lennon conjured the track through the distorting mirror of a Leslie speaker, to evoke the unearthly distance between dreamworlds and reality. At one point, Harrison added some subtle flickers of backward guitar between Lennon's vocal lines. Desperate for inspiration, the group even turned to a group of fans waiting loyally outside the studio, picking two teenage girls who claimed they could sing, and layering their voices like a choir of tarnished angels over Lennon, Harrison, and McCartney's harmonies.

But even after further tinkering on 8 February, Lennon pronounced himself dissatisfied—though not, it seems, through lack of effort from the other Beatles. Leaving McCartney and Harrison to claim the two sides of the upcoming single, Lennon consigned his song to a charity LP being prepared for the World Wildlife Fund by comedian Spike Milligan.

The album had not yet appeared by January 1969, so Lennon assumed that the song was there for the (re)taking: "We may as well stick it on here," he noted dryly, "rather than waste it." In a rare show of outward enthusiasm during the Twickenham sessions, George Harrison attempted to persuade Lennon that the February 1968 version was nothing less than superb.

It was certainly more successful than their attempts in January: John couldn't remember any of the words, and had to send a messenger to music publisher Dick James in search of the official lyrics registered for copyright purposes. Meanwhile, the group went ahead desultorily, turning in a succession of labored renditions that parodied the song's flowing imagery. After 9 January, "Across the Universe" was duly abandoned.

Later that week, Apple announced that Lennon's song—in its February 1968 form, of course—would be featured on a forthcoming Beatles EP, alongside the four "new" songs that had been buried on the otherwise uninspired *Yellow Submarine* soundtrack album. Spike Milligan immediately reminded Lennon that he'd promised the track to the World Wildlife Fund, and that its commercial appeal would be eradicated if it had already appeared on a Beatles record. Remixed, substantially speeded up, and overdubbed with sound effects by George Martin, "Across the Universe" became the lead track on the charity LP *No One's Gonna Change My World* in December 1969.

By then, Michael Lindsay-Hogg's final cut of the *Let It Be* movie had been completed, featuring some damning footage of the group's inspiration-free assault on "Across the Universe." Given the task of upgrading his initial *Get Back* lineup, Glyn Johns borrowed back the February 1968 tape of the song and set about creating a "new" version, which might sound like an offcut from the January 1969 sessions. He removed George Martin's overdubs, as well as the vocal harmonies added by the Beatles and their fans in 1968.

That was in early January 1970. Two months later, Phil Spector took over the project, and he returned to the February 1968 mix. Whereas George Martin had speeded up this tape, Spector slowed it down, before adding strings, brass, a choir, and Ringo Starr's drums, all during a tempestuous session at Abbey Road on 1 April 1970. This hyperbolic, excessively lush arrangement appeared on *Let It Be,* and has passed into history as the "official" Beatles version of the song.

I Me Mine
(GEORGE HARRISON)
RECORDED 3 JANUARY 1970;
1, 2 APRIL 1970

"You hear something, and it registers in your mind as something else," George Harrison explained on the morning of 8 January 1969, as he played Paul McCartney his newly written waltz, "I Me Mine." As he'd watched a BBC TV documentary about the British honors system the previous evening, a piece of incidental music in three-quarter time had fitted the rhythm of a phrase that was running through Harrison's head.

"It's about the ego, the central problem," the composer explained in his autobiography a decade later, and given that much of 7 January had been devoted to a bitter argument about roles and ground rules within the Beatles, it's not difficult to imagine that Harrison had a particular set of egos in mind.

In his autobiography, which he named after this song, he widened the connotations, explaining how the experience of taking LSD had dissolved his personal ego into a collective, spiritual force he called "the big 'I'; i.e. OM, the complete whole, universal consciousness that is void of duality and ego."

Returning from that realization to the everyday pettiness of individual needs, "suddenly I looked around, and everything I could see was relative to my ego—you know, like 'that's my piece of paper' and 'that's my flannel,' or 'give it to me' or 'I am.' It drove me crackers; I hated everything about my ego—it was a flash of everything false and impermanent which I disliked." Hence the song, with its title proclaiming the dominance of the ego: "I Me Mine." The two simple verses of lyrics, bound to an Italianate waltz structure, expressed the universality of ego in the material world: "All through the day, I me mine / All through the night, I me mine." And all through the Twickenham sessions, as Harrison was only too aware.

For all that, McCartney's ego was sufficiently submerged on 8 January 1969 to encourage and support the rehearsal of "I Me Mine"—though Lennon was less generous. He first suggested that George's song would make a good TV commercial, then complained that the chords were too difficult to play (Harrison schooled him gently through them) and that anyway the song was too short.

McCartney mended that problem by leading the group into an improvised, up-tempo middle section. Paul's gratis addition created a song out of what was, until then, little more than a fragment. Michael Lindsay-Hogg's cameras caught a little of this process, documenting Harrison's first acoustic rendition of the verses and then a full electric take by George, Paul, and Ringo, while Lennon and Yoko Ono watched from the dance floor. No sooner had the song been perfected than it was dropped from the sessions.

Just as Lennon's "Across the Universe" had to be recalled from limbo for the soundtrack album, so "I Me Mine" was resurrected for Glyn Johns's January 1970 *Get Back* LP. On 3 January, the same three-man Beatles lineup strolled through the recording of the song at Abbey Road, complete with vocal, organ, and guitar overdubs. "I Me Mine" was still hardly an epic—it now ran for ninety-four seconds in total—but it was included on the second acetate of *Get Back* (and, in 1996, on *Anthology 3*).

When Phil Spector was recruited to prepare the final *Let It Be* album, he concocted an extended version of "I Me Mine" by simply copying and inserting one of the verses and the middle eight into the track. The splices were masked with string, brass, and choral overdubs on 1 April 1970. The contrast between the synthetic grandeur of the verses and the stark, thrilling edge of the middle section was one of Spector's grand coups on the album.

Dig It
(JOHN LENNON/PAUL MCCARTNEY/
GEORGE HARRISON/RICHARD STARKEY)
RECORDED 26 JANUARY 1969

"Can you dig it?" The Beatles didn't just dig it, they simply adored this slice of late '60s hippie slang, and incorporated it into their conversations and their jam sessions during January 1969. Their relentless improvisation on 8 January, which could be titled "Get Off," hinged around endless repetition of the phrase. And during the final week of sessions at Apple, "Can You Dig It?" or "Dig It" was given as a title to four different but consistently uninspired jams.

On 24 January, Lennon concluded one such electric ramble with a line of dialogue that eventually made its way onto the *Let It Be* LP: "That was 'Can You Dig It?' by Georgie Wood. Now we'd like to do 'Hark the Angels Come.'" Two days later, the Beatles and Billy Preston romped through a twelve-minute, three-chord improvisation led by an exuberant

Lennon, who spewed out meaningless lyrics like a hip ticker-tape machine: "You can dig it in the morning, dig it every day, dig it in the evening, dig it every way you want it." He also called out the names of blues guitarist B. B. King, actress Doris Day, and British soccer manager Matt Busby.

Glyn Johns selected this portion of the performance for both the *Get Back* LPs he prepared, in May 1969 and January 1970. Less than a minute of the jam was eventually slipped onto Phil Spector's final mix of the *Let It Be* album. Fortunately, perhaps, two further "Dig It" jams, on 27 and 29 January respectively, weren't officially recorded.

Let It Be
(JOHN LENNON/PAUL MCCARTNEY)
RECORDED 31 JANUARY 1969;
30 APRIL 1969; 4 JANUARY 1970

"I think it was inspired by 'Bridge over Troubled Water,'" John Lennon reckoned in one of his final interviews. In fact, Paul Simon's equally self-conscious spiritual ballad was composed after this Paul McCartney song, the undoubted creative peak of the January 1969 sessions. Both writers drew on the same gospel-soul tradition, epitomized by America's leading R&B vocalist of the late '60s, Aretha Franklin—who appropriately enough recorded both "Let It Be" and "Bridge over Troubled Water" before the summer of 1970.

During one of the Twickenham sessions, McCartney pegged Franklin as a direct influence on "Let It Be," which he had begun to write during the final sessions for *The White Album* in the fall of 1968. Its stately piano chords were reminiscent of that summer's "Hey Jude," but nothing McCartney had composed to date matched the dignified spirit of this song.

Having completed the framework of the piece by the end of 1968, McCartney was understandably proud of his handiwork. On 8 January 1969, he demonstrated the song to the other Beatles, inspiring no response at all from George Harrison, mild interest from Ringo Starr, and an outbreak of gentle sarcasm from John Lennon, who noted the apparently religious imagery about "Mother Mary" in the chorus and suggested that McCartney should substitute "Brother Malcolm" (for road manager Mal Evans) instead.

The next day, substantial progress was made, as Lennon picked ambiguously at a bass guitar and joined Harrison for some erratic har-

Paul (background) working on "Let It Be" while George takes a break.
COURTESY OF PHOTOFEST

monies. Still a verse or two short of a song, McCartney ad-libbed his way through the lyric, though such lines as "Read the *Record Mirror,* let it be" were hardly destined to be keepers.

During the hiatus between the Twickenham and Apple sessions that month, McCartney painfully completed a second verse, but when Glyn Johns was ready to tape the song on 26 January, the third verse remained unfinished (*Anthology 3* has the evidence). Only on 31 January was the final lyric in place—in its way a counterpart to Lennon's "Across the Universe." But while the latter stressed the thrill of succumbing to the subconscious, McCartney's words viewed it as a source of comfort and acceptance, a reservoir of calming memories that could have both personal and universal significance.

Throughout its lyrical development, the song's arrangement scarcely altered, though there were minor changes—the Beatles dropped the idea of accompanying McCartney's piano intro, for instance. When the final run-throughs were staged in front of the cameras on 31 January, a series of virtually perfect, and virtually identical, takes were taped and filmed, but Harrison's guitar solo remained a sticking point. On 30 April 1969, George overdubbed a replacement that at least gave the impression of having been thought out. During the early January sessions in 1970, a second solo, altogether more confident and aggressive, was added to the multitrack, giving subsequent remixers an option to spare. Also taped at that session were some discreet brass and cello overdubs, scored by George Martin.

For his first lineup of *Get Back* in May 1969, Glyn Johns had obviously used the 30 April guitar overdub. Strangely, he made the same decision when he revamped *Get Back* on 5 January 1970—just twenty-four hours after the guitar, brass, and string overdubbing had taken place. By ignoring the Beatles' own change of heart, he surely contributed to the rejection of his second shot at the soundtrack LP—leaving open the door for Phil Spector.

The American producer intervened too late to be involved in the release of "Let It Be" as a single, which took place in March 1970 and featured the mix prepared by George Martin for the Beatles on 4 January. For the album, though, Spector substituted the January 1970 guitar solo and accentuated the percussion to the point that it began to seize attention from the lyric. "I think Phil maybe got a little too fruity on that one,"

Lennon commented later—his only public criticism of Spector's judgment on this project.

Maggie Mae
(TRADITIONAL, ARRANGED BY JOHN LENNON/PAUL MCCARTNEY/GEORGE HARRISON/RICHARD STARKEY)
RECORDED 24 JANUARY 1969

During their late '50s schooling as skiffle musicians, the Beatles often drew on traditional folk and blues tunes for their repertoire. Skiffle stars Lonnie Donegan, the Vipers, and Johnny Duncan all built their reputation on souped-up arrangements of songs that had been in the public domain for decades. Without their example, it is unlikely that the Beatles would ever have learned—or indeed remembered—"Maggie Mae," a Liverpool folk tune about a prostitute and a robbery.

On 24 January 1969, the Beatles made three separate attempts to busk their way through the adventures of Maggie and her encounters with the Merseyside police. After the second, they signaled to Glyn Johns that he should tape them next time. Sadly, their third rendition rapidly broke down, but the Beatles never returned to the song. Nonetheless, this "Maggie Mae" fragment survived every revamping of the *Get Back/Let It Be* album, okayed by the group, Johns, and Phil Spector alike as a perfect snapshot of these supposedly impromptu sessions.

I've Got a Feeling
(JOHN LENNON/PAUL MCCARTNEY)
RECORDED 30 JANUARY 1969

More than a decade after the teenage musicians first proudly scrawled the line "Another Lennon/McCartney original" under a set of lyrics in a school exercise book, "I've Got a Feeling" brought their active songwriting collaboration to an end.

Alone of all the new material on the *Let It Be* album, this song seems to have been completed and arranged before the January 1969 sessions began. Like "A Day in the Life" before it, "I've Got a Feeling" combined separate song fragments from Lennon and McCartney. Lennon's primary contribution was the "Everybody Had a Hard Year" section in the latter half of the song.

That fragment—a bleak, almost self-pitying dirge originally hung on two simple chords—dated from December 1968. Alongside "A Case of the Blues" and a pitiful lament called "Oh My Love," it was written at Lennon's home, Kenwood, in the aftermath of the loss of his first child with Yoko Ono, John Ono Lennon II. Yoko suffered her miscarriage in late November, a few weeks after the couple was busted on drug charges. Harassed by the police and the press, grieving for their lost son, and now flirting with heroin abuse, Lennon and Ono can be forgiven for turning inward in a maudlin outpouring of paranoia and pain.

In its original form, "Everybody Had a Hard Year" was unrelievedly dark. But by early January, Lennon had toned down the imagery, replacing anguish with ambivalence. "Everybody pulled their socks up," he sang defiantly, "everybody put the fool down." No prizes for guessing which role he saw himself playing.

In context, Lennon's lines were softened by being placed inside a McCartney song of compelling power but virtually no lyrical content. Its moody blues changes and exaggerated vocals hid the emptiness of its words: the couplet "Oh please believe me, I'd hate to miss the train / And please believe me, I won't be late again" was hardly a cry from the heart. But the song's middle section, delivered in a voice raw enough to sour milk, served as a brutal declaration of love for Linda Eastman—an ironic counterpoint to the rapid deflation of Lennon and Ono's romantic dreamscape.

During Harrison's and Lennon's brief exchange of work in progress at the start of the Twickenham sessions, John fitfully demonstrated "I've Got a Feeling"—or, at least, "Everybody Had a Hard Year" plus his dimly remembered idea of what McCartney was contributing to the song. Paul corrected him later in the day, suggesting that the two men had briefly collaborated on the arrangement a few weeks earlier. Harrison, meanwhile, introduced an early sense of tension by pointing out similarities between the guitar riff of Lennon/McCartney's new song and Otis Redding's "Hard to Handle." "That doesn't matter," Lennon snapped in reply.

The fusion having coalesced without apparent effort, the Beatles eased themselves into the basic structure of the song, returning to it whenever the atmosphere at Twickenham was threatening to sour. But as the *Let It Be* movie illustrated, there was still room for dissension. The dispute between Harrison and McCartney over the descending guitar riff out of the middle section didn't spark the row glimpsed in the movie, but it remained a contentious point until the end of the January sessions. More often, though, "I've Got a Feeling" was a celebration of Beatles unity—even when Lennon, as on 9 January, was so confused by their lack of progress that he couldn't remember whether he was supposed to sing on this number or not. As it turned out, with both John and Paul vocalizing, "I've Got a Feeling" was a highlight of the rooftop performance at Apple on 30 January. That rendition appeared in the *Let It Be* movie and on the LP. As contrary as ever, Glyn Johns opted for a faltering 24 January recording for his two shots at compiling the *Get Back* LP. "I cocked it up trying to get loud," Lennon confessed as the song broke down—an admission preserved when this take was included on *Anthology 3*.

The One after 909
(JOHN LENNON/PAUL MCCARTNEY)
RECORDED 30 JANUARY 1969

During a month scarred with bad feeling, most of it unresolved, one song transported the Beatles back to a time when they were a single, unified force, capable of trouncing every rock band on Merseyside. "The One after 909" was one of the earliest Lennon/McCartney compositions, dating from around 1959. It was certainly completed by the time the group went to Hamburg for the first time in 1960, and it remained in their repertoire until well into 1963. That spring, in fact, it was briefly considered as a follow-up single to "Please Please Me," before being jettisoned in favor of the newly composed "From Me to You."

For such a simple song, it had an unusual structure, deliberately eschewing the twelve-bar blues format that might have been its natural mode. "We always thought it wasn't finished," Lennon remarked on 3 January 1969, which was when it reentered the Beatles' orbit. McCartney noted that "our kid [his brother Michael] has been saying that we should do that for years," and that he'd always laughed him down. The young Beatles might have been embarrassed by its nonlinear narrative and fake American imagery, but by January 1969, any sense of innocence was welcome. Of all the songs played at Twickenham and Apple that month, "The One after 909" delighted everyone who heard it—not least because it seemed to act as a four-man tranquilizer.

Once they'd settled on the loosest of arrangements and incorporated Billy Preston's electric piano into the ensemble, the song remained unchanged. Their one and only rendition from the Apple rooftop caught its nonchalance and humor so perfectly that Glyn Johns chose it as the first track on both lineups of his *Get Back* album.

The Long and Winding Road
(JOHN LENNON/PAUL MCCARTNEY)
RECORDED 31 JANUARY 1969;
1 APRIL 1970

Lennon's lack of creativity during the January 1969 sessions was brought into sharp relief by the fact that McCartney contributed two of his most durable ballads to the *Let It Be* album: the title track and this song, which had again been under construction in the closing weeks of 1968. During one of the final *White Album* sessions, in fact, McCartney taped a solo piano demo of the song, still unfinished, as a present for the wife of Apple aide Alistair Taylor, who'd expressed his admiration for the melody.

It's surprising, then, that McCartney coyly held the song back during the first few Twickenham sessions. Finally, he could wait no longer: on 7 January, he demoed the song—or at least the chorus and the one verse he'd completed—for studio onlookers. The next day, he began to teach it to Harrison and Starr, Lennon being otherwise involved with Yoko Ono.

But it was only during the final days of the month, at Apple, that he succeeded in persuading the other Beatles to attempt the song. Even when the final version was recorded on 31 January, Lennon's shockingly mediocre bass guitar line effectively sabotaged the performance. As *Anthology 3* (where this take was included, albeit misdated 26 January) made clear, Lennon had difficulty maintaining both tempo and key on this instrument.

Because his *Get Back* album was supposed to be an audio vérité documentary of the January 1969 sessions, Glyn Johns had no option other than to settle for the best of the 31 January takes. But given carte blanche to improve the "truth" for *Let It Be,* Phil Spector made the momentous decision to drown "The Long and Winding Road" in lush strings and a choir who sounded as if they were on loan from an amateur production of *King of Kings.* The overdubs successfully concealed the inadequacies of Lennon's bass work, while Spector also removed McCartney's monologue during Billy Preston's keyboard solo and Paul's showy piano finale.

"I don't think there is anything that you can point to in the Beatles records I made that wasn't tasteful," George Martin asserted in *Melody Maker* in 1971, "But 'The Long And Winding Road' was BBC-TV music, like Mantovani and the Mike Sammes Singers." The song's composer also professed outrage at the surgery, even going so far as to cite Spector's "butchery" as a significant factor in the breakdown of relations between the ex-Beatles during 1970.

John plays a slide on "For You Blue."
COURTESY OF PHOTOFEST

For You Blue
(GEORGE HARRISON)
RECORDED 25 JANUARY 1969

The surviving audiotapes from the Twickenham sessions in early January 1969 provide a depressing insight into the relationship between George Harrison and his senior colleagues, Lennon and McCartney. During the month, Harrison tentatively introduced a series of songs that had the potential to outstrip anything Lennon brought to the sessions—among them "All Things Must Pass," "Isn't It a Pity," and "Let It Down"—only to find his delicate creations derided or just ignored.

Early in the proceedings, he seems to have taken a conscious decision to present the other Beatles only with songs that would require little effort on their part, which is why the *Let It Be* album featured two of his shortest and most simple numbers: "I Me Mine" and "For You Blue." With Lennon, in particular, apparently unwilling to learn any Harrison song requiring more than a vague knowledge of three chords, George's palette was understandably restricted.

Like "I Me Mine," "For You Blue" was brought to the group the morning after it was composed. As Harrison piped his way through the song's facile twelve-bar structure and banal lyrics, Lennon and McCartney chatted among themselves. No wonder that a few minutes later Harrison declared his unwillingness to let the Beatles perform any of his songs on their live show, because "they'll turn out shitty."

He enjoyed more success, albeit not with Lennon, the next day, when the other Beatles deigned to perform "I Me Mine." Flushed by this triumph, he arrived at Twickenham on the morning of 9 January determined to force a second song on the group. Briefly, his attempt worked: Lennon picked at an electric guitar, McCartney coaxed bluesy trills out of the piano, and Starr settled into a comfortable groove. Then McCartney switched their attention to "Two of Us," and the moment was lost.

So, like "I Me Mine," "For You Blue" was effectively begun and finished in a single day—this time at Apple on 25 January, by which time the presence of Billy Preston had imposed a level of good behavior on the group. Ironically, though, Preston was absent during the brief period the group allotted to Harrison's song. Instead, McCartney contributed excellent honky-tonk piano, while Lennon essayed some surprisingly competent bottleneck guitar. Glyn Johns alighted on the day's final take for his *Get Back* album, and with some minor vocal overdubs (presumably carried out at the start of the Phil Spector sessions the following year), that performance was carried forward to the *Let It Be* LP. The undubbed original surfaced twenty-six years later on *Anthology 3*.

Get Back
(JOHN LENNON/PAUL McCARTNEY)
RECORDED 27 JANUARY 1969

Few Beatles songs have been the subject of so much retrospective controversy—not for the ambiguity of their lyrics, with vague references to transsexuality (a full year before the Kinks' "Lola"), but for McCartney's original intention in writing the song. "Every time he sang the title in the studio," John Lennon claimed in *Playboy* in 1980, "he'd look at Yoko. Maybe he'll say I'm paranoid." So might anyone who views the *Let It Be* film, where Lennon enters into the song with more gusto than you'd expect from a man who suspects that his girlfriend is being insulted during every performance.

"I originally wrote it as a political song," McCartney explained late during the January 1969 sessions, prompting a sarcastic suggestion for a title from George Harrison: "How about 'Councillor McCartney Tells Them Where It's At'?" A sample verse from the composer's original improvised lyric was published in 1970 as part of the brief text in the *Get Back* book included with early British copies of the *Let It Be* LP. "Don't dig no Pakistanis taking all the people's jobs," it began—enough, two decades later, for a London daily newspaper to denounce McCartney as a racist and a supporter of the right-wing politician Enoch Powell, who had led a prominent campaign in the late '60s demanding that immigrants of ethnic origin, from Asia and the Caribbean, should be deported to avoid civil strife.

As prominent supporters of black music throughout their careers, proselytizers on behalf of Indian culture, and regular campaigners against any form of discrimination, the four Beatles were among the unlikeliest racists in Britain. McCartney's short-lived "Don't dig no Pakistanis" verse was actually intended as political satire, an attempt to translate Powell's rhetoric into song and make it appear ridiculous. Satire being a dangerous weapon, and McCartney not being a natural politician, it is perhaps just as well that his original plan didn't survive for more than a day or two in January 1969.

The song's moment of creation can be dated precisely to early in the morning rehearsal on 7 January 1969, when McCartney was vamping through blues riffs on his bass guitar while waiting for Lennon to arrive. During his improvisation he hit upon a lick that's recognizably the seed of "Get Back"—and pursued it, first as a rhythm, then with a melody busked over the top. Within forty-eight hours, it had acquired a chorus, a title, and a lyric that named not only Pakistanis but Puerto Ricans and (bizarrely) Mohicans—who weren't exactly heavily represented in the British population of 1969.

During an otherwise fruitless session on 13 January, McCartney and Lennon set themselves the task of writing a sensible lyric—or at least a nonpolitical one—based around a character called Jo-Jo, who ended up hailing from Tucson, Arizona, purely because McCartney had visited the city the previous year, to view a farm he'd considered buying. "It's where they shoot *The High Chaparral*," he explained to the others, citing a popular TV drama of the time. But without Harrison, still sulking in Esher, the Beatles' efforts to nail the song proved fruitless.

When the sessions shifted to Apple, "Get Back" rapidly became the focus, not least because it was the song that showed the most commercial potential. On 23 January, Ringo Starr abandoned a drum pattern that had been restraining the rhythm, and adopted a driving beat that effectively underpinned and powered the song. As McCartney still struggled to turn the lyrics into a story, he conceded that he'd "never really been stuck" the original words; he'd just liked the sound of "Pakistani." Meanwhile, Lennon graciously handed over to Billy Preston one of the two guitar solos he'd been allowed, with the frank admission that "I'll only be able to work one out." The arrangement was settled by the next day, and on 27 January the group recorded the superb performance that was issued as a single in April—although with a coda glued on from another take on 28 January. On the rooftop at Apple two days after that, "Get Back" was both the first and last song to be performed; as seen in the movie, the final rendition was interrupted by members of the Metropolitan Police, just as Paul had fantasized early in the Twickenham sessions. It was included on *Anthology 3* for historical rather than musical reasons.

ABBEY ROAD

Come Together
(John Lennon/Paul McCartney)
Recorded 21, 22, 23, 25, 29, 30
July 1969

Acid guru Timothy Leary was one of those who flocked to the Lennons' bedside during their Toronto bed-in for peace in May 1969. The two men shared more than an all-consuming zeal for psychedelic chemicals: both were actively seeking a new world order, although Lennon's benign vision of universal goodwill was altogether more sedate than Leary's excited visions of a planet running on LSD rules. Dr. Leary was after more than comradeship in Toronto. He planned to run for elective office in the United States—the higher the better—and who better to concoct a campaign song than the man who'd openly admitted that acid was the inspiration behind many of his finest songs? Leary even had a title ready: "Come Together."

"So Tim Leary asked me to write a song," Lennon recalled in *Playboy* before his death. "I tried and I tried, but I couldn't come up with one. But I came up with my 'Come Together,' which would have been no good to him." Guiltily, Lennon didn't abandon his commission there, though neither man was satisfied with the banal ditty—"Come together / Join the party"—which the Beatle sheepishly sang down a phone line that fall.

Instead, Lennon was left with his song, apparently written between his car accident at the start of July 1969 and his return to London a week later. "They're very Lennon lyrics," commented George Harrison sagely in *Disc* at the time, which wasn't surprising: in their own oblique way, they were strictly personal. If the song's title was an overtly sexual reference, the lyrics were a sly self-portrait in clipped, obtuse images.

Sometimes the references were only too obvious: "He bag production / He got walrus gumboat / He got ono sideboard" cleverly alluded to his newly formed company, one of his most famous Beatles songs, and his wife in turn. But elsewhere, as when he boasted, "He got early warning," the message was less clear. Was Lennon really proud of his halitosis?

Ultimately, it didn't matter. "I like the sound of the record," Lennon said gleefully, while Harrison tagged it "one of the nicest things we've done, musically. It's an upbeat, rockabeataboogie."

The whispered vocal tag of "shoot me" took on an eerie new significance after 1980, while the opening line of lyrics ("Here come old flat-top /

He come grooving up slowly") had an alternate life of its own, having been borrowed from Chuck Berry's car-chase song "You Can't Catch Me." Lennon acknowledged the steal, but claimed to *Playboy* it was irrelevant: "It's nothing like the Chuck Berry song, but they took me to court because I admitted the influence once. I could have changed it to 'Here come old iron face,' but the song remains independent of Chuck Berry or anybody else on earth."

But the line remained, and the consequences spiraled down the years. The legal effects were still being felt in 1975, by which time Lennon had agreed to cover several Berry songs, initially reneged on his agreement, then obliged, then signed over the rights to the album on which they were placed, then fought in court to get the rights back again. If he'd changed the offending line in 1969, neither *Rock and Roll* nor *Roots,* both released in 1975, would ever have been recorded.

Though both Lennon and Harrison praised the finished record, and George noted that "Ringo's drumming is great," "Come Together" suffered more than anything else on *Abbey Road* from George Martin's shortcomings as a rock producer. When the Beatles listened to the Band's debut album, *Music from Big Pink,* they were amazed by Levon Helm's drum sound. "Why can't we sound like that?" they quizzed Martin. But as the pinprick percussion on "Come Together" showed, their producer didn't know the answer.

The *Anthology 3* compilation includes the initial take of the song, on which Lennon's voice was raw and unechoed, as he pushed the band forward in an attempt to squeeze time. "Eartha Kitt, man," he quipped over the fade-out. The finished record—painstakingly assembled over ten days of sessions—retained some of that sleazy blues feel.

Something
(GEORGE HARRISON)
RECORDED 2, 5 MAY 1969; 11, 16 JULY 1969; 15 AUGUST 1969

"Something in the way she moves" is one of the most famous first lines in pop history, but it wasn't written by George Harrison. It was actually the title, and opening lyric, of a song by James Taylor, who recorded it in the summer of 1968—for the Beatles' Apple Records label. Harrison was briefly involved in the James Taylor LP sessions and must have heard "Something in the Way She Moves" before its commercial release in December that year.

Nonetheless, the Beatle was struck by the haunting implications of the phrase, and he borrowed it, one must assume deliberately, as the introduction to his most famous song. He'd apparently begun to explore its possibilities as early as October 1968—engineers at the *White Album* sessions recall hearing him busking a tune of that title—but he didn't begin serious work on the song until late January 1969. "I sort of put it on ice," he explained later, "because I thought, 'This is too easy. It sounds so simple.'"

During one of the final *Get Back* sessions at Apple, Harrison strummed through the chords, and admitted that he had reached a lyrical blank after the first line. Surprisingly, neither Lennon nor McCartney took the opportunity to exclaim, "And you nicked that one!" Instead, the band gingerly rehearsed the chord sequence, while Lennon (in a rare spirit of generosity toward Harrison) began to suggest lyrical possibilities. George completed the lyric a week or two later—"the words are nothing, really," he announced that fall—and then, as he did with "All Things Must Pass" and "My Sweet Lord" in 1970, initially failed to notice the potential of his own best work. Convinced that the song wasn't worth offering to the Beatles, he taped a solo electric demo (available on *Anthology 3*) on his twenty-sixth birthday in late February, at which point the lyrics had gained an extra verse, declaimed during the space left for the solo. He then scouted around for a suitable recipient. "I almost passed it to [Apple artist] Jackie Lomax," he explained to *Melody Maker* in late 1969, "but I really imagined someone like Ray Charles doing it. So I gave it to Joe Cocker instead."

Cocker taped the song that spring, no doubt unaware that, in the meantime, Harrison had decided to present it to the Beatles after all. They (minus Lennon, who as usual opted out of a Harrison session) cut the song's backing track on 16 April 1969, then scrapped it and began again on 2 May. This time Lennon condescended to play rhythm guitar, as the three-minute song uncoiled until it lasted almost eight minutes, extended by a simplistic instrumental jam. "We kept on playing it over and over," Harrison complained to the *New Musical Express* at the end of the year, "until we played it so much that I didn't know what it was. I listen to it now, [and I know] I could do a whole lot better."

Work resumed on "Something" in mid-July, without Lennon, when Harrison overdubbed a replacement vocal and chopped some of the dross from the instrumental coda. A twenty-one-piece string orchestra was added to the track on 15 August, and the following week the song was trimmed down to its final length, eradicating all memory of the extraneous instrumental work.

Almost universally greeted as his finest work to date—even George had to admit to *Disc* it was "probably the nicest melody I've ever written"—"Something" benefited from a lyric that was both universal and painfully personal. "You're asking me, will my love grow," he sang, "I don't know." Within a few months, his marriage to model Patti Boyd was under threat from his close friend Eric Clapton.

Confessional lyric or not, "Something" proved to be the greatest triumph of Harrison's career to date. It was chosen as his first Beatles A-side—albeit shared with "Come Together." More prestigious still, it entered the repertoire of Frank Sinatra, who patted George on the back with one hand by introducing it on stage as "the greatest love song ever written," and then knifed him with the other by regularly giving the credit to Lennon/McCartney.

Maxwell's Silver Hammer
(JOHN LENNON/PAUL McCARTNEY)
RECORDED 9, 10, 11 JULY 1969;
6 AUGUST 1969

"I hate it," declared John Lennon in *Playboy* just before his death, "because all I can remember is the track. Paul made us do it a hundred million times. He did everything to make it a single, and it never was, and it never could have been. We spent more money on that song than any of them in the whole album."

Even in 1969, George Harrison admitted that "Maxwell's Silver Hammer" "was one of those instant, whistle-along tunes which some people will hate, and others will love." Among the latter was its composer, Paul McCartney, who devoted every possible second of the *Get Back* and *Abbey Road* sessions to a novelty tune as suitable for children as the Grimms' fairy tales. "It's sort of sick," Harrison declared to the *New Musical Express* when he was ostensibly promoting *Abbey Road*. "The guy keeps killing everybody."

"The guy" was one Maxwell Edison, whose unlikely exploits as a serial killer are the subject of one of McCartney's most idiosyncratic songs. He introduced it to his unsuspecting colleagues on 3 January 1969, guiding them through the chord sequence (as seen in the *Let It Be* film). Four days later, Maxwell was back, this time immediately after an argument that had come close to splitting the band. This song might have been the final straw, but instead its banality seemed to calm the Beatles' nerves, especially when roadie Mal Evans was recruited to bang an anvil with a hammer, more or less in time with the chorus. McCartney drove them through the song again the next day, and he even persisted after Harrison's departure on 10 January. Then, mercifully, "Maxwell's Silver Hammer" was laid aside until the sessions were over.

It reappeared on 9 July—which just happened to be John Lennon's first day back in the studio after his car crash. Three full days of Maxwell's exploits followed, Ringo manning the anvil this time, before the song was ready for Moog synthesizer overdubs in early August—which at least gave George Harrison, who controlled the knobs since it was his machine, some belated satisfaction. Take Five, from 9 July, was included on *Anthology 3* in 1996, complete with a guide vocal from McCartney and some minimal accompaniment.

Oh! Darling
(JOHN LENNON/PAUL McCARTNEY)
RECORDED 20, 26 APRIL 1969;
17, 18, 22, 23 JULY 1969;
8, 11 AUGUST 1969

The White Album was rock's first postmodern record, a self-conscious history of pop's progress from the Jazz Age to the Vietnam War. Its aura of affectionate pastiche survived in this song, which Paul McCartney began to write during the final sessions for the double LP.

Despite constant comparisons over the last twenty-eight years, "Oh! Darling" has nothing beyond a similar title in common with the 1958 Ritchie Valens hit "Oh Donna." Stylistically, it's far closer to the Fats Domino canon, its piano triplets and mournful air reminiscent of '50s classics like "Blueberry Hill," "I Want to Walk You Home," and "Walking to New Orleans," yet without plagiarizing any of them.

"If he'd had any sense, he would have let me sing it," opined John Lennon in one of his less gracious interviews. "It was more my style than his. He didn't sing it too well." No doubt there was more than a slice of jealousy behind Lennon's comment, a barbed compliment for the accuracy of its '50s references.

Lennon seems to have heard the skeleton of the song before the Twickenham rehearsals began, and by 7 January the Beatles were tentatively approaching the tune—George Harrison steering them into another New Orleans R&B standard from the '50s, "One Night (Of Sin)," whenever the middle section approached. McCartney drifted into the simple piano chords several times at Twickenham, but he didn't bother to push the song too hard when the sessions switched to Apple in late January.

So "Oh! Darling" was set aside, reappearing at the *Abbey Road* sessions in April. Lennon wasn't allowed near a microphone on 20 April 1969, but was deputed to play organ. Unusually, the Beatles reverted to their 1963 methods for this track, playing and singing the entire song live in the studio; an early take is featured on *Anthology 3*. McCartney's lead vocal was a purr rather than a roar, and he made five separate attempts to improve it in April and then mid-July before capturing the throat-shredding performance heard on *Abbey Road*. Even then the track wasn't complete: dissatisfied with Harrison's rather tentative lead guitar part, McCartney replaced it with his own in August.

Octopus's Garden
(RICHARD STARKEY)
RECORDED 26, 29 APRIL 1969;
17, 18 JULY 1969

Ringo Starr's songwriting was a standing joke within the Beatles. As early as 1963, he'd announced the imminent completion of a tune called "Don't Pass Me By," but until 1968, every melodic fragment that he performed shyly for the other Beatles was greeted with howls of laughter, as his colleagues pointed out exactly which Jerry Lee Lewis or Johnny Cash country standard he'd plagiarized this time.

Composing wasn't as central to Ringo's self-image as it obviously was for George Harrison, but he was suitably delighted by the fact that the song he'd been working on for five years had been included on *The White Album*. Early in the Twickenham sessions, he'd demonstrated the bare structure, and clichéd melodies, of two virtually identical songs called "Taking a Trip to Carolina" and "Picasso." Three weeks later, at Apple, he had a new composition to perform for John Lennon: one verse of "Octopus's Garden," inspired by his first experience diving off the coast of Sardinia during a holiday the previous fall.

On 26 January 1969, as glimpsed in the *Let It Be* movie, George Harrison heard the fragment for the first time. With a generosity of spirit he probably wouldn't have mustered for McCartney or Lennon, he effec-

Ringo.
COURTESY OF PHOTOFEST

tively rewrote the song at the piano, structuring the chord sequence and linking together the verses, while Lennon rattled out accompaniment on the drums.

Typically, Harrison found spiritual depth in Starr's vision of innocent pleasure beneath the waves: "On the surface, it's a daft kids' song, but I find the lyrics very meaningful. It's [a] deep meaning which Ringo probably doesn't even know about—the lines about 'resting our heads on the sea bed,' and 'we'll be warm beneath the storm.' It makes me realise that when you get deep into your consciousness, it's very peaceful. Ringo writes his cosmic songs without knowing it." (*New Musical Express.*)

The Beatles virtually completed the song in a single session, on 26 April 1969 (see *Anthology 3*), though the backing vocals and Harrison's lead guitar solo were perfected at a later date. "Octopus's Garden" emerged as a charming, guileless piece for children of all ages, without any of the forced naiveté that had made "Maxwell's Silver Hammer" such a struggle to record.

I Want You (She's So Heavy)
(JOHN LENNON/PAUL McCARTNEY)
RECORDED 22, 23 FEBRUARY 1969;
18, 20 APRIL 1969;
8, 11, 20 AUGUST 1969

Yoko Ono wielded a dramatic influence over John Lennon's songwriting after 1968. Central to her manifesto was the belief that simplicity was richer than metaphor. The lyricist who'd jumbled together madcap images of chaos and confusion in songs like "I Am the Walrus" and "Happiness Is a Warm Gun" virtually disappeared: the new Lennon recognized that bare emotions required the minimum of verbiage.

"I Want You (She's So Heavy)" illustrated the point perfectly. Its lyric sheet was scarcely longer than its title—naked lust in the first phrase, a stunned admission that he'd been overpowered in the second. "It has John playing lead guitar," George Harrison revealed in the *New Musical Express* at the time, "and singing the same as he plays." Even basic harmonies were irrelevant in the presence of overwhelming emotion.

Lennon first toyed with the rhythm of the song, and its title, late in the Twickenham sessions; he later acknowledged that Mel Tormé's mid-'60s pop hit "Coming Home Baby" had been his original inspiration. Its hook was not verbal but musical: a relentless, multidubbed guitar riff that, as Harrison admitted, proved that "John has an amazing thing with his timing. Yet when you question him about it, he doesn't know. He just does it naturally, and you can't pin him down."

The first of the *Abbey Road* songs to be started, in late February 1969 at Trident Studios, "I Want You (She's So Heavy)" was originally intended to flesh out the *Get Back* album. At first, the song was required to stand alone; the dramatic climax, the battalion of Lennon/Harrison guitars, was added only in mid-April.

Bizarrely, Lennon returned to the February tape when he began to tinker with the mix in August. Added that month were a sea of white noise from a Moog synthesizer, which coated this paean of desperate lust with an unearthly menace, and the three-part vocal harmonies that introduced the guitar riff. On 20 August, segments of both the April and August versions of the same basic track were edited together to form the *Abbey Road* track—the join is clearly audible four and a half minutes into the song—while the guitar riff was sliced to a stop with brutal finality. Nothing else in the Beatles' catalog looks forward so clearly to the vision that fueled Lennon's remarkable *Plastic Ono Band* album in 1970.

Here Comes the Sun
(GEORGE HARRISON)
RECORDED 7, 8, 16 JULY 1969;
6, 11, 15, 19 AUGUST 1969

The early summer nightmare of business machinations and confrontational meetings that scarred 1969 may have opened an unbridgeable chasm between Lennon and McCartney. But for George Harrison, they had one happy, and financially beneficial, consequence. "During that time, when we had all those meetings," he explained to the BBC that winter, "I used to get these dreadful headaches, just sitting there, listening to all this rubbish. So one day I stayed off, like skiving off school, and I went to Eric Clapton's house instead, because it's nice, with trees and things. It was obviously a release from the tension that had been building up. I picked up the guitar for the first time in a couple of weeks, because I'd been so busy—and the first thing that came out was 'Here Comes The Sun.'"

Built around a series of variations on a simple D-major chord, irresistible for anyone with an acoustic guitar in hand, "Here Comes the Sun" clearly came from the heart. "It's been a long hard lonely winter," Harrison sang. The coming of summer brought the promise of freedom.

For once, George didn't have to expose his optimism to Lennon's cynicism, since there is no evidence that John was actually in the studio during any of the long sessions devoted to "Here Comes the Sun" in July and August 1969. If he had been, he might have noted the similarity between this song title and his own "Here Comes the Sun King," which had first surfaced at the Twickenham sessions in January.

The three-man Beatles cut the basic track on 7 July; McCartney and Harrison overdubbed the harmony vocals a day later; and Harrison himself handled the addition of harmonium and some delicate flourishes from his Moog synthesizer. Then in mid-August, George layered several more guitar parts over the song, which was then decorated with a string and woodwind section arranged by George Martin. That "Here Comes the Sun" could still sound so uncluttered was a testament to its melodic strength.

Because
(JOHN LENNON/PAUL McCARTNEY)
RECORDED 1, 4, 5 AUGUST 1969

Anxious to hammer home Yoko Ono's artistic credentials in April 1969, John Lennon announced to the *New Musical Express* that "she trained as a classical musician. I didn't know that until this morning. In college she majored in classical composition. Now we stimulate each other like crazy. This morning I wrote this song called 'Because.' Yoko was playing some classical bit, and I said 'Play that backwards,' and we had a tune." "Some classical bit" proved to be Beethoven's "Moonlight Sonata," which even when played backward "still sounds like Beethoven," as George Harrison duly noted.

With its pantheistic spirituality and openness toward the rest of mankind, "Because" was an unexpected Lennon composition to come out of the uneasy spring of 1969. It caught exactly the same mood of peace and contentment that the maharishi's meditation camp had instilled in McCartney the previous year, enabling him to write the equally wide eyed "Mother Nature's Son." Yet Lennon was writing "Love is all" while his group and his business empire were crumbling around him and he was shadowed by the constant specter of heroin abuse. "The lyrics speak for themselves," he explained to *Playboy* shortly before his death. "They're clear. No bullshit, no imagery, no obscure references."

The Beatles stopped short of inviting Yoko Ono to repeat her piano exercises in the studio. Instead, George Martin fingered the theme on an electric harpsichord, while Lennon doubled the melody on electric guitar. But the heart of the recording was the group's finest display of vocal harmonizing ever: a three-part arrangement for the "lead," and then two further layers of voices as accompaniment. George Martin revealed that "I was literally telling them what notes to sing"; George Harrison confessed that "the harmony was very difficult to do." But the effort was worthwhile. Harrison rated it his favorite track on *Abbey Road,* and "one of the most beautiful things we've ever done." So impressive was the vocal arrangement that the instruments were stripped from the track for airing at an audiovisual presentation about the Beatles at Abbey Road in the early '80s, an effect repeated for *Anthology 3* in 1996.

You Never Give Me Your Money

(JOHN LENNON/PAUL MCCARTNEY)
RECORDED 6 MAY 1969; 1, 11, 15, 30, 31 JULY 1969; 5 AUGUST 1969

On 6 May 1969, in the middle of the savage battle between the Beatles and ATV over the future of Northern Songs, Paul McCartney introduced a new song to the group's repertoire. Under the circumstances, its message could hardly have been more straightforward: "You never give me your money, you only give me your funny paper, and in the middle of negotiations, I break down."

This being the songsmith McCartney, and not the minimalist Lennon, "You Never Give Me Your Money" didn't end with its haunting opening verse. In fact, it shifted through five distinct sections in less than four minutes, each further removed from its original subject. In effect, the finished track was not just the introduction to the legendary *Abbey Road* medley but a medley in itself.

In its original form, the track ran for nearly six minutes, the final two devoted to a dadaist instrumental jam reminiscent of the extended fade of "Strawberry Fields Forever." During a series of overdub sessions in July, this manic, hilarious ending was excised, while the group added harmony vocals. McCartney stripped out his original bass part in favor of a far more inventive line, which dominated the latter stages of the track. Then, on 30 July, "You Never Give Me Your Money" was segued into the opening moments of "Sun King"—though later editing made the transition more abrupt, when the organ drone that opened "Sun King" was deleted.

Sun King

(JOHN LENNON/PAUL MCCARTNEY)
RECORDED 24, 25, 29 JULY 1969
(WITH "MEAN MR MUSTARD")

During the Beatles' stay in India in the spring of 1968, fellow transcendental meditation student Donovan taught John Lennon a new finger-picking technique for acoustic guitar. Lennon carried the method into his songwriting over the next year, basing "Julia" and "Look at Me" around similar guitar figures. At the end of that year, another variant on the technique emerged as the skeleton of "Sun King." At the first Twickenham session in January 1969, Lennon unveiled nothing more than a riff and a title, which blended smoothly into another song in progress, "Don't Let Me Down."

"He used to call it 'Los Paranoias,'" George Harrison revealed to the *New Musical Express* that year, but it was as "Here Comes the Sun King" that this delicate ballad was first recorded in late July 1969. From the start, it was taped as part of a medley, the transition to the starkly contrasting "Mean Mr Mustard" announced with a fusillade of drums.

"That's a piece of garbage I had around," Lennon noted dolefully in *Playboy,* but it was garbage dressed in the finest jewelry. Like "Because," it was decorated with some sublime vocal harmonies, and a starry-eyed refrain: "Everybody's laughing, everybody's happy." A late addition was the parade of nonsense lyrics that closed the song, owing something to Spanish, something to Italian, and more to the delight in wordplay that had triggered Lennon's first two books.

Mean Mr Mustard

(JOHN LENNON/PAUL MCCARTNEY)
RECORDED 24, 25, 29 JULY 1969
(WITH "SUN KING")

"I'd read something in the newspaper about this mean guy who hid five-pound notes, not up his nose but somewhere else," Lennon explained to *Playboy* in 1980. Like the news stories that inspired "A Day in the Life," this vignette from life's stranger side mutated into a Beatles song—in the unlikely surroundings of the maharishi's camp in Rishikesh. Lennon taped the song during the demo sessions for *The White Album* on their return (*Anthology 3* has the evidence), but the Beatles began to rehearse it only on 8 January 1969, at which point its composer was still stressing that it was unfinished. It briefly reappeared as part of a medley with the improvised "Madman" on 14 January, before being recorded in a more lasting combination with "Sun King" in July. Throughout its eighteen-month gestation, the song remained unchanged in every way but one: Mr. Mustard's sister's name changed from Shirley to Pam once the Beatles decided on the next song in the medley.

Polythene Pam
(JOHN LENNON/PAUL MCCARTNEY)
RECORDED 25, 28 JULY 1969
(WITH "SHE CAME IN THROUGH THE BATHROOM WINDOW")

Like "Mean Mr Mustard," "Polythene Pam" was written in India in 1968, and recorded in July 1969 as part of a medley, this time with "She Came in through the Bathroom Window." Delivered in a thick Scouse accent by Lennon, the song recalled "a little event with a woman in Jersey, and a man who was England's answer to Allen Ginsberg. I met him when we were on tour, and he took me back to his apartment. He had a girl he wanted me to meet. He said she dressed up in polythene. I just sort of elaborated [it], into perverted sex in a polythene bag. I was just looking for something to write about."

Though some of Lennon's wilder vocal interjections were edited out of the finished record, "Polythene Pam" remains the most Liverpudlian performance the Beatles ever recorded. It flowed into a rasping Harrison guitar solo, which in turn triggered the segue into the medley's next segment.

She Came in through the Bathroom Window
(JOHN LENNON/PAUL MCCARTNEY)
RECORDED 25, 28 JULY 1969
(WITH "POLYTHENE PAM")

As the only Beatle with a house in central London during the '60s, Paul McCartney occasionally came home after a session to discover that over-zealous fans had rifled through his drawers in search of souvenirs. Though John Lennon reckoned that the song was actually inspired by Linda Eastman—"He wrote that when we were in New York announcing Apple, and we first met Linda. Maybe she was the one who came in the window"—McCartney affirmed that the theft of clothes and personal effects inspired him. "This is something that happened to me quite recently," he deadpanned during an early attempt to cut the song.

It had clearly been suggested as a candidate for *The White Album,* because the entire group seemed familiar with its structure when McCartney introduced it to the Twickenham rehearsals on 6 January

1969. The next day, it proved to be just about the only song that the Beatles could play right through without error, though Harrison's inability to reach the high harmony caused a few problems.

Boredom had begun to set in by 9 January, when Paul flogged the group through a lengthy series of rehearsal takes. Only two verses were complete by this point, leaving him to improvise a third about the British comedy artiste Danny La Rue. Further rehearsals on 22 January proved no more productive, and McCartney filed the song away for the next album. As the take on *Anthology 3* illustrated, the song was now fleshed out to three verses and a middle eight, but lacked any sense of urgency.

That was supplied when "Bathroom Window" followed "Polythene Pam" in late July 1969, its place in the *Abbey Road* medley already secure. McCartney was convinced of its commercial potential; like George Harrison's "Something," this song was given to Joe Cocker several months before the Beatles completed work on their own rendition.

Golden Slumbers
(JOHN LENNON/PAUL McCARTNEY)
RECORDED 2, 3, 4, 30, 31 JULY 1969;
15 AUGUST 1969
(WITH "CARRY THAT WEIGHT")

On "The Inner Light," George Harrison had created a musical setting for an Indian spiritual text. With "Golden Slumbers," McCartney composed a new tune for a lullaby by the English poet and dramatist Thomas Dekker—being unable to read the sheet music that carried the original seventeenth-century melody.

Retaining almost all of Dekker's words, McCartney succeeded in concocting a tune that sounded like a dimly remembered favorite from childhood. Along with "Carry That Weight," with which it seems to have been connected from the outset, he demonstrated it to Ringo Starr at Twickenham in January 1969. But the two songs weren't recorded until July, with George Martin adding a mighty orchestral accompaniment the following month.

Carry That Weight
(JOHN LENNON/PAUL McCARTNEY)
RECORDED 2, 3, 4, 30, 31 JULY 1969;
15 AUGUST 1969
(WITH "GOLDEN SLUMBERS")

Accidentally or not, McCartney composed his own theme song for the January 1969 sessions: "Boy, you're gonna carry that weight a long time."

So it proved for the rest of the year, and he accentuated the point during the July recording of the song by

incorporating the main lyrical and musical theme from "You Never Give Me Your Money."

The first mix of "Golden Slumbers"/"Carry That Weight" had no orchestra, and had solo vocals—with McCartney bellowing the repeated chorus of "Carry That Weight" like a drunken laborer. On the finished record, three Beatles contributed unison vocals to the refrain; appropriately, Lennon was absent from that session.

The End
(JOHN LENNON/PAUL MCCARTNEY)
RECORDED 23 JULY 1969;
5, 7, 8, 15, 18 AUGUST 1969

What became known in the studio as "The Huge," or the Medley that filled most of the second half of *Abbey Road,* required a conclusion; hence yet another set of McCartney fragments were transformed into "The End." Though it seemed to fit seamlessly onto the record after "Carry That Weight," it was actually an entirely separate recording. The original track featured neither the vocals nor the series of short guitar solos (allotted to McCartney, Harrison, and Lennon, in that order) that dominated the final version. "The End" also included Ringo Starr's first drum solo on record, and a lavish orchestral finale. (It didn't, however, ever conclude with the piano chord added to a remix on *Anthology 3;* that extraneous keyboard effect was purloined from the session tape for "A Day in the Life," from February 1967.)

The first lyric that Paul concocted for the song was pure doggerel, but the second was acknowledged by Lennon as "a very cosmic, philosophical line": "And in the end, the love you make is equal to the love you take." It served as a verdict on both the idealism of the '60s and the disintegration of the Beatles.

Her Majesty
(JOHN LENNON/PAUL MCCARTNEY)
RECORDED 2 JULY 1969

Several of the songs on the second side of *Abbey Road* were unfinished fragments. McCartney's "Her Majesty" had been debuted on piano, vaudeville style, during the Twickenham sessions. At Apple, on 24 January 1969, he transferred the song to guitar, while Lennon floundered on electric slide. But although that rendition stretched for two painful minutes, it simply repeated the single verse that provided an unexpected ending to *Abbey Road*—originally hidden, uncredited, after "The End."

Its presence there was entirely due to EMI engineer Malcolm Davies, who saved it at the end of a tape reel after McCartney decided that it didn't fit in its original slot (between "Mean Mr Mustard" and "Polythene Pam"). Paul asked for it to be discarded, but Davies knew better, and after it took McCartney by surprise as the master reel spooled to a close, he suggested that the finished record should end the same way.

THE REVIEWS

Accustomed to awed enthusiasm from the media, the Beatles were taken unawares in 1967 when rock acquired its own aesthetic, and critics unafraid to employ it. Richard Goldstein's legendary pan of *Sgt. Pepper* in the *New York Times* marked the first occasion on which the group had been publicly attacked by a member of the rock community. The Beatles expected, maybe even relished, uncomprehending attacks from older showbiz writers. But intelligent critiques from journalists overtly aligned with the so-called counterculture were more difficult for them to accept.

In Britain, where there was little evidence of rock writing until the early '70s, *Abbey Road* was greeted with almost unanimous praise. In the best-selling pop paper of the era, *New Musical Express,* Alan Smith acclaimed the album's "beautiful blistering music," which "exceeds the double album . . . parts of it touch the heights of *Sgt. Pepper.*" Smith laid down a defiant challenge: "Show me any other group packing so much originality of composition and honest pop music onto one album."

In the United States, the staff of *Rolling Stone* was no longer convinced that "honest pop music" was enough. Divided over the album's merits, the magazine took the unusual step of running parallel reviews to reflect the critical gulf. Ironically, John Mendelssohn and Ed Ward came close to matching the Beatles' own response to *Abbey Road:* McCartney, Starr, and George Martin relished its invention and skill; Lennon damned its insignificance. Much of Ward's rhetoric about the relative importance of unpolished rock played on "real instruments" and synthetic, orchestrated pop could have been pulled directly from Lennon's legendary interview with Jann Wenner at the end of 1970. In the London *Times,* meanwhile, classical critic William Mann—an early champion of the group—provided a dewy-eyed encapsulation of the public response to *Abbey Road.*

The reception of *Let It Be* the following year was inevitably tarnished by the bootleg versions of the Glyn Johns acetates circulating since the previous fall. For the first time in rock history, critics could judge the "official" release of a new album alongside an earlier, rejected version. Primed by the bootlegs to expect a record without any studio trickery, they were prepared to reject *Let It Be* on ethical grounds alone. Less attention was paid to the songs than to their production, and Phil Spector was universally named as the prime suspect—even taking the rap for the Beatles' own decisions, like the horn overdubs onto "Let It Be."

This time, Britain and the United States were in near agreement. John Mendelssohn, the champion of *Abbey Road,* responded to *Let It Be* with the bitterness of a betrayed disciple: note his revised judgment on "Oh! Darling" since the previous year. In the *New Musical Express,* Alan Smith mirrored Mendelssohn's outrage, and his critical assault typified the British response to the album. Once again, William Mann in the *Times* demonstrated his uncanny ability to discover merit in the Beatles' work, in the most unpromising of circumstances.

Abbey Road

Rolling Stone
15 November 1969
by John Mendelssohn

Simply, side two does more for me than the whole of *Sgt. Pepper,* and I'll trade you *The Beatles* and *Magical Mystery Tour* and a Keith Moon drumstick for side one.

So much for the prelims. "Come Together" is John Lennon very nearly at the peak of his form; twisted, freely associative, punful lyrically, pinched and somehow a little smug vocally. Breathtakingly recorded (as is the whole album), with a perfect little high-hat-tom-tom run by Ringo providing a clever semi-colon to those eerie shoo-ta's.

George's vocal, containing less adenoids and more grainy Paul tunefulness than ever before, is one of many highlights on his "Something," some of the others being more excellent drum work, a dead catchy guitar line, perfectly subdued strings, and an unusually nice melody. Both his and Joe Cocker's version will suffice nicely until Ray Charles gets around to it.

Paul McCartney and Ray Davies are the only two writers in rock and roll who could have written "Maxwell's Silver Hammer," a jaunty vaudevillian/music-hallish celebration wherein Paul, in a rare naughty mood, celebrates the joys of being able to bash in the heads of anyone threatening to bring you down. Paul puts it across perfectly with the coyest imaginable choir-boy innocence.

Someday, just for fun, Capitol/Apple's going to have a compile a Paul McCartney Sings Rock and Roll album, with "Long Tall Sally," "I'm Down," "Helter Skelter" and, most definitely, "Oh! Darling," in which, fronting a great "ouch!"-yelling guitar and wonderful background harmonies, he delivers an induplicably strong, throat-ripping vocal of sufficient power to knock out even those skeptics who would otherwise have complained about yet another Beatle tribute to the golden groovies era.

That the Beatles can unify seemingly countless musical fragments and lyrical doodlings into a uniformly wonderful suite, as they've done on side two, seems potent testimony that no, they've far from lost it, and no, they haven't stopped trying.

No, on the contrary, they've achieved here the closest thing yet to Beatles free-form, fusing more diverse intriguing musical and lyrical ideas into a place that amounts to far more than the sum of those ideas.

I'd hesitate to say anything's impossible for the Beatles after listening to *Abbey Road.* To my mind they're equalable, but still unsurpassed.

Rolling Stone
15 NOVEMBER 1969
BY ED WARD

Eeeeeeeeeeeeek, it's the Beatles. Look. Look. They're crossing Abbey Road in London—John all leonine and scrunched up and dressed in white with tennis shoes, and Ringo in a tux, and Paul out of step with the others (what do you suppose that means?), and George looking very intense and with much better posture than the others. Up the block a ways a police van is watching, but it's cool because they're crossing in the pedestrian crossing area and I'm sure that thing Paul is carrying is a Players—they're playing it very safe. A nice yellowish colored picture on one of those nice new instant fall-apart covers. Sixteen new Beatles songs for just under seven bucks.

What's it like? Well, I don't like it much, but then I don't have a thing about the Beatles. Since *Revolver* I've been buying their albums, playing them a couple of times, and then forgetting about them. The last album was, admittedly, exciting in places, but I still don't play it much because there's still too much stuff on it that should have been edited. Singles are a different matter, since for some reason they are more exciting, but the albums just don't seem very vital. They are masterpieces of the engineer's art, containing a melodic gift that is rare these days, and occasionally, lyrics that are truly excellent. In fact, about as close to perfect as one can come in this field. And as Crosby, Stills & Nash have shown, perfection can be carried to the point of sterility, yet the Stones are close to perfect and anything but sterile.

Part of the reason can be found, I think, in a comparison of the production techniques used by the Beatles and Stones. The Beatles create a sound that could not possibly exist outside of a studio. Electronically altered voices go "la la la" in chorus, huge orchestras lay down lush textures, and the actual instruments played by the Beatles themselves are all but swallowed up in the process. Indeed, *Abbey Road* is the address of a studio in London. On the album, tape splices go whizzing by, and the ear strains to dissect layers of overdubbing. For the first time they play with their new Moog, which disembodies and artificializes their sound. Too often the result is complicated instead of complex.

In direct contrast with this we have the Stones. They all play real instruments and exactly at that. Additional instrumentation seems to be used only when there is no alternative and then it is kept to the minimum and mixed in unobtrusively. They, too, spend a lot of time remixing and overdubbing, but the end result is always credible—one can imagine little Stones performing in the speakers. The tape splices are there, but it is hard to tell just where, and the one time they really overextended themselves on record, *Their Satanic Majesties Request*, is looked upon as pretty much of a failure for just that reason. After that, they got a producer to help keep them in check and went back to making good music. I wonder what the Beatles would sound like if Jimmy Miller produced them?

Of course, the Beatles are still the Beatles, but it does tread a rather tenuous line between boredom, Beatledom, and bubblegum. "Come Together," the first track, is a superb bit of Lennonian babbling about such things as toejam football and mojo filter which contains such memorable lines as "got to be good looking 'cause he's so hard to see," and "hold you in his armchair, you can feel his disease." It's all very catchy, very funny, and quite mad, all of which is just fine with me.

Unfortunately, it is followed by "Something," by George Harrison, which *Time* magazine says is the best song on the album, and it's sure easy to see why. It's got a nice, easy-listening melody, vapid lyrics and a gigantic string section oozing like saccharine mashed potatoes all over the place. The vocal is comparable to Glen Campbell in the fervor of its delivery. It's so vile that I'm sure it will be covered by eight or ten artists in the next month and will rate with "Yesterday" and "Michelle" as one of the Fab Four's top money makers.

Things get a little better (it couldn't get worse) with the next cut, "Maxwell's Silver Hammer," about a guy named Maxwell Edison, a student majoring in medicine, who goes around killing people. It's all done as a nice bouncy catchy little song, quite hummable and singable, sort of like something left over from *Sgt. Pepper* and featuring some pale imitation Buddy Holly vocal hiccups. It's cute and pretty well done, but not particularly memorable.

Side two is a disaster, although it begins well enough with George's "Here Comes The Sun," a pleasant number with lots of Top 40 appeal, even if the lyrics are nothing special. The arpeggios at the end, along with those at the end of the last song on the first side, are motifs that keep cropping up throughout the rest of the album. At first I thought that this might indicate some unifying and thematic thread running throughout all the little songs at the end, but that doesn't seem to be the case.

The slump begins with "Because," which is a rather nothing song, featuring lots of little Ellington saxophone-voiced Pauls singing harmonies that are not unlike the Hi-Los. The backing, lyrics, everything but the vocal, sounds like the Bee Gees, but it's not—it's the Beatles. "You Never Give Me Your Money" is a song with so many sections that it never gets anywhere, but the biggest bomb on the album is "Sun King," which overflows with sixth and ninth chords and finally degenerates into a Muzak-sounding thing with Italian lyrics. It is probably the worst thing the Beatles have done since they changed drummers. This leads into the "Suite" which finishes up the side. There are six little songs, each slightly under two minutes long, all of which are so heavily overproduced that they are hard to listen to and only two of which have decent melodies—

"Golden Slumbers" which features a large string section, but doesn't suffer for it, and "Carry That Weight" which is quite infectious. The side closes with the obligatory funny trick (it's not over when you think it is), and there you are.

Now, much has been made of the "get back" phenomenon, with so many artists eschewing the complicated and returning to roots of one kind or another. It is ironic that the Beatles should have put out a single with that advice, as well as an admonition not to let them down, followed that advice quite well with the follow-up record, and then released an album like this. We're told that their next one will be all Beatles playing instruments with no overdubbing or any of the other things that mar *Abbey Road* so badly. It is tempting to think that the Beatles are saying with this album that the only alternative to "getting back" for them is producing more garbage on this order, and that they have priced it so outrageously so that fewer people would buy it. But if that's so, then why bother to release it at all? They must realize that any album they choose to release is going to get a gold record just because so many people love, respect and trust the Beatles. They've been shucking us a lot recently, and it's a shame because they don't have to. Surely they must have enough talent and intelligence to do better than this. Or do they? Tune in next time and find out.

The Times (London)
5 DECEMBER 1969
"THOSE INVENTIVE BEATLES"
BY WILLIAM MANN

If adverse reviews elsewhere have dissuaded you from buying *Abbey Road*, the Beatles' new LP, do not hesitate any longer. It teems with musical invention—mostly by Lennon and McCartney, though all four contribute songs—and the second side, as a piece of musical construction, is altogether remarkable and very exciting, indeed. The stereo recording will be called gimmicky by people who want a record to sound exactly like a live performance: how can that guitarist (presumably George Harrison) in "Here Comes The Sun" hop three or four yards sideways so quickly? He can't, but the effect is agreeable and adds a non-visual drama to the music. Like the back-tracked horns in "Maxwell's Silver Hammer", and the electronic distortion of the voice in "Oh! Darling", the stereo manipulation is used for a musical purpose, not just to make the sound ravey.

The first two songs on side one, "Come Together" and Harrison's "Something", have been put out as a single. Nice as they are—especially the lazy ostinato bass in the former—they are minor pleasures in the context of the whole disc. For mass appeal I would have pinned greater hopes on "Maxwell", a neo-vaudeville comic song about a jocular murderer, and Ringo Starr's "Octopus's Garden", which might be called Son of Yellow Submarine and, like "Maxwell", delights the teenybopper in all of us. Side one ends with a long piece, "I Want You", which is really two alternating tunes: the second of these (actually heard first as an instrumental prelude), "She's So Heavy", is built on a haunting ground-bass that eventually monopolises a grand build-up, in the manner of "Hey Jude", growing and proliferating and getting louder until the only solution was to cut the tape dead when the side is full. Most exciting.

But not as marvellous as side two. This begins with Harrison's slow, torrid "Here Comes The Sun", much the most powerful song he's written so far, only hinted at for the moment. It melds into "Because", not Guy d'Hardelot but Lennon-McCartney, mind-blowing close harmony (it reminds me of "This Boy" all those years ago, though the harmonies are more subtle nowadays) over an asymmetrical 3 plus 5 rhythmic pulse. Then a wistful tune, "You Never Give Me Your Money", with a down-to-earth second half in honky-tonk style that fades into a further instalment of "Sun King" with words in a mixture of Spanish and Italian. This blends into a whole series of rock 'n' roll songs that seem to find their tunes in developments of the same initial mood and musical invention.

Some have called this a medley but the effect is more dramatic, more structural; to tie the music further together there is even a back-reference to the ground-bass of "She's So Heavy". The last portion of the side begins softly with a new tune to the old words "Golden slumbers kiss your eyes"; towards the end of the Beatles' double LP there was a send-up ballad called "Goodnight", and "Golden Slumbers" is a companion to it, but straight rock ballad, not send-up cyclamate.

It merges into a new refrain with a heavy rock beat, "Boy, you're gonna carry that weight", and this includes a reprise, with full symphony orchestra, of the "You Never Give Me Your Money" tune that got lost a long way earlier: its return is as satisfying as the discovery of a ten-bob note you've been missing for a week. The tempo steps up for a one-line tune that never gets as far as line two because guitar and drums go off on their own in an inspired duet until quick piano chords introduce the last song-epigram: "And in the end the love you take is equal to the love you make". The record seems to be over but the long pause is followed by a mini-tribute to "Her Majesty" in which voice and guitar walk slowly across the room.

A pity the words of the songs aren't supplied with the record. John Lennon has said that *Abbey Road* is an attempt to get away from experiment and back to genuine rock 'n' roll, so I suppose they don't want us to study the words: a pity because learning by ear isn't as accurate. In any case, when anyone is as naturally inventive as the Beatles, to try non-experimentation is a forlorn hope.

LET IT BE

The Times (London)
8 MAY 1970
"STRONG AS EVER" BY WILLIAM MANN

Ghoulish rumour-mongers are putting it about that *Let It Be* is the Beatles' last LP together, and this is why the record sleeve, accompanying book (much too fat to be called a booklet) and outer cover are black-edged, and may be why the album costs so much. Let us attend the funeral when life is pronounced extinct: at the moment the corporate vitality of the Beatles, to judge from *Let It Be*, is pulsating as strongly as ever.

The album takes its title from a recent single written by Lennon and McCartney, performed here in a slightly more elaborate version; *Let It Be* is also the title of the new Beatles film to be shown later this month. The fat book of colour photographs and conversations is called *The Beatles Get Back,* slightly confusing since "Get Back" is another recent Beatles single (also included, a little abbreviated, on the LP) and was, for a time, the projected name of the film. All will be sorted out eventually, no doubt.

Meanwhile the LP is a sort of trailer for the film's music. As such it does not attempt any large-scale musical construction such as distinguished side two of *Abbey Road;* there are, on the other hand, several very short tracks, snatches of music that may recall things in Paul McCartney's solo LP. Of the 12 tracks there are two by George Harrison, one fragment of a rude Liverpool song about Maggie Mae, another fragment, "Dig It", ascribed to all four Beatles, and the rest are by Lennon and McCartney.

The first of the two sides is the stronger, containing at least three lovely new songs. "Across the Universe" follows the manner of "Strawberry Fields" and "Glass Onion", worthily so. The refrain, "Nothing's gonna change my world", is really haunting, and the instrumentation (with acoustic guitars and a distant choir) has great character—but this is true of other tracks as well, and the stereo placing of sound is consistently fascinating. "Dig A Pony" has a captivating refrain too, as well as relaxed, imaginative harmony and construction. George's "I Me Mine", a slow rock number, took my fancy immediately with its easy switches of musical metre.

As we may now expect, there is a slow ballad by Paul, "The Long And Winding Road", good of its kind, perhaps not specially distinctive. Also on the second side is a pleasant 12-bar blues by George, "For You Blue", which features Hawaiian effect and some chat during the music; and an early Lennon-McCartney, "One After 909", recorded now for the first time. A slowish, quiet blues called "I've Got A Feeling" has that gently insinuating quality of some other Lennon-McCartney songs ("Let It Be" is another) which at first seem ordinary but gradually take complete possession of the listener's inner ear. Not a breakthrough record, unless for the predominance of informal, unedited live takes (Phil Spector is the producer); but definitely a record to give lasting pleasure. They aren't having to scrape the barrel yet.

New Musical Express
9 May 1970
"New LP Shows They Couldn't Care Less" by Alan Smith

If the new Beatles' soundtrack album *Let It Be* is to be their last then it will stand as a cheapskate epitaph, a cardboard tombstone, a sad and tatty end to a musical fusion which wiped clean and drew again the face of pop music. At £3—bar a penny—can this mini-collection of new tracks, narcissistic pin-ups and chocolate box dressing really be the last will and testament of the once-respected and most-famous group in the world?

What kind of contempt for the intelligence of today's record-buyer is it that foists upon them an album at this price with seven new tracks; two bits of dressing in the shape of "Dig It" and "Maggie May" [*sic*]; and the three previously-released numbers "Let It Be", "Get Back" and "Across the Universe"?

I suspect, in fact, that almost £1 of the cost is to cover the accompanying book of fab glossy pix . . . and lump it or leave it, music lovers.

On the reckoning of this album the Beatles have in any event lost their self-respect and sold out all the principles for which they ever stood.

Remember all those quotes about "the men in suits" and the contempt for candyfloss Hollywood chorales, and the earnest pride in their albums, and the fervent yearning to reject phoneyness right along the line? Forget it . . . because with this LP, the philosophy seems to be exactly one of hype in a pretty packet.

The Beatles are, or were, about music—not the waffle surrounding and enclosed with *Let It Be*. And it pains me to see them go along, or accept, this load of old flannel and musical castration.

The tragedy is that what little remains of the original album (this set ties in with the soundtrack of the documentary film *Let It Be*) is some of the best straight rock the Beatles have recorded in years.

Almost all of the fun and raw feel has been taken away or polished up by Phil Spector, who was called in by Allen Klein to give a nice professional 're-production' to the LP, but he does leave in Lennon's intro to the opener, "Two Of Us".

"I Dig A Pygmy, by Charles Hawtrey and the Deaf Aids," bawls Lennon. "Phase one, in which Doris gets her oats."

Doris' oats turn out to be a kind of honey-soft rocker about going home, sung by McCartney with, I think, Lennon harmonising. And if McCartney and Lennon ever get dark days of nostalgia about their past, then this is the one for the record-player.

Next is the short Lennon "Dig A Pony" ("you can penetrate any place you go"); then Lennon's ethereal and beautiful "Across the Universe", in which he sings that "nothing's gonna change my world."

Following track is George's Russian-flavoured "I Me Mine", a strong ballad with a frantic centre; then it's Lennon's "Can You Dig It", which is no more than a few seconds of a smile-raising chant about a number of items from the FBI to Matt Busby; then McCartney with a version of "Let

It Be"; and then another few seconds of the old Liverpool ballad of "Maggie May" [*sic*].

Side Two starts with a good McCartney rocker, "I've Got A Feeling", with cymbals, screams and Lennon coming in with a hushed-voice refrain about "having a good time and putting the floor down" [*sic*]. Both this and the follower, "One After 909", are excellent stuff in which McCartney and Lennon really work together.

Next is a predictably beautiful ballad from McCartney, "The Long And Winding Road"—and I can understand why he should object to the heavenly choir and other trimmings which were added without his permission.

In its original form, this song had empty simplicity. Now it's all obtrusive Mantovani-type strings and Cinemascope chorale . . . acceptable . . . but totally unnecessary.

The worst development in the fortunes of the Beatles is that whereas their finances may be one thing, interference in their individual work without control—as in "Long And Winding Road"—is something else altogether.

Final tracks are another strong one from George, a whispery chunky rocker called "For You Blue" ("Elmore James," he calls out at one point, "got nothin' on this baby"); and then "Get Back".

The worst thing about the excellent live numbers on this album is that there are so few of them. The next worst thing is that they are dressed up in an abundance of glossy card and paper and pushed out at £3 minus one penny.

The tragedy is that on the strength of the little new music there is on this LP, the Beatles were never informally better, never more with their feet on the ground.

George Harrison believes the Beatles will work together again and, if only to restore the respect of those who admire, appreciate and love them, I pray he is right.

I have followed, vaunted and glowed with Merseyside pride at the achievements of the Beatles since the pre-"Love Me Do" days of the Blue Angel and New Brighton Tower.

But in its overwrapped state, this glorified EP is a bad and sad mistake.

Rolling Stone

11 JUNE 1970

BY JOHN MENDELSSOHN

To those who found their work since the white album as emotionally vapid as it was technically breathtaking, the news that the Beatles were about to bestow on us an album full of gems they'd never gotten around to polishing beyond recognition was most encouraging. Who among us, after all, wouldn't have preferred a good old slipshod "Save The Last Dance For Me" to the self-conscious and lifeless "Oh! Darling" they'd been dealing in?

Well, it was too good to be true—somebody apparently just couldn't *Let It Be,* with the result that they put the load on their new friend P. Spector, who in turn whipped out his orchestra and choir and proceeded to turn several of the rough gems on the best Beatles album in ages into costume jewelry.

Granted that he would have preferred to have been in on the project from its inception rather than having it all handed to him eight months after its announced release date (in which case we would never have been led to expect spontaneity and his reputation would still be intact), one can't help but wonder why he involved himself at all, and wonder also, how he came to the conclusion that lavish decoration of several of the tracks would enhance the straightforwardness of the album.

To Phil Spector, stinging slaps on both wrists.

He's rendered "The Long And Winding Road," for instance, virtually unlistenable with hideously cloying strings and a ridiculous choir that serve only to accentuate the listlessness of Paul's vocal and the song's potential for further mutilation at the hands of the countless schlockmongers who will undoubtedly trip all over one another in their haste to cover it. A slightly lesser chapter in the ongoing story of McCartney as a facile romanticist, it might have eventually begun to grow on one as unassumingly charming, had not Spector felt compelled to transform an apparently early take into an unextravaganza of oppressive mush. Sure, he was just trying to help it along, but Spectorized it evokes nothing so much as dewy-eyed little Mark Lester warbling his waif's heart amidst the assembled Oliver orchestra and choir.

"I Me Mine," the waltz sections of which remind one very definitely of something from one of *The Al Jolson Story*'s more maudlin moments, almost benefits from such treatment—it would have been fully as hilarious as "Good Night," after all, had Spector obscured its raunchy guitar with the gooey strings he's so generously lavished on the rest of it. As he's left it, though, it, like "Winding Road," is funny enough to find cloying but not funny enough to enjoy laughing at.

Elsewhere, Spector compounds his mush fixation with an inability to choose the right take (it is said that nothing on the "official album" comes from the actual film sessions, mind you). Inexplicably dissatisfied with the single version of "Let It Be," for instance, he hunted up a take in which some jagged guitar and absurdly inappropriate percussion almost capsize the whole affair, decided that it might be real Class to orchestrally embellish the vocal, and thus dubbed in—yes!—brass. Here the effect isn't even humorous—Spector was apparently too intent on remembering how the horns went on "Hey Jude" to listen closely enough to this one to realize that they're about as appropriate here as piccolos would have been on "Helter Skelter."

Happily though, he didn't impose himself too offensively on anything else, and much of what remains is splendid indeed:

Like John's "Across the Universe," which, like "Julia," is dreamy, childlike, and dramatic all at once and contains both an unusually inventive melody and tender devotional vocal.

Like the two rough-honed rockers, the crudely revival-ish "I've Got A Feeling" and "One After 909," both of which are as much fun to listen to as they apparently were to make. "C'mon, baby, don't be cold as ice" may be at once the most ridiculous and magnificent line Lennon-McCartney ever wrote.

Like John's crossword-puzzlish "Dig A Pony," which features an urgent old rocker's vocal and, being very much in the same vein as such earlier Lennonisms as "Happiness Is A Warm Gun," nearly makes up for the absence of "Don't Let Me Down" and "The Last Dance." And especially everyone's two favorites, "Two Of Us," which is at once infectiously rhythmic and irresistibly lilting in the grand tradition of "I'll Follow The Sun," and the magnificent chunky, thumping, and subtly skiffly "Get Back," which here lacks an ending but still contains delightful camping by John and Billy Preston.

All of these are, of course, available on the bootleg versions of the album, a further advantage of which is their pure unSpectoredness and the presence of various goodies that didn't quite make it to the official release.

Musically, boys, you passed the audition. In terms of having the judgement to avoid either over-producing yourselves or casting the fate of your get-back statement to the most notorious of all over-producers, you didn't. Which somehow doesn't seem to matter much any more anyway.

DISCOGRAPHY

Abbey Road

U.S.: Apple SO 383 (released 1 October 1969)
U.K.: Apple PCS 7088 (released 26 September 1969)

Side 1: *Come Together / Something / Maxwell's Silver Hammer / Oh! Darling / Octopus's Garden / I Want You (She's So Heavy)*

Side 2: *Here Comes the Sun / Because / You Never Give Me Your Money / Sun King / Mean Mr Mustard / Polythene Pam / She Came in through the Bathroom Window / Golden Slumbers / Carry That Weight / The End / Her Majesty*

Let It Be

U.S.: Apple AR 34001 (released 18 May 1970)
U.K.: Apple PCS 7096 (released 8 May 1970)

Side 1: *Two of Us / Dig a Pony / Across the Universe / I Me Mine / Dig It / Let It Be / Maggie Mae*

Side 2: *I've Got a Feeling / The One after 909 / The Long and Winding Road / For You Blue / Get Back*

The original U.K. edition included the *Get Back* book of photographs by Ethan Russell and text by Jonathan Cott and David Dalton.

Get Back / Don't Let Me Down

U.S.: Apple 2490 (released 5 May 1969)
U.K.: Apple R 5777 (released 11 April 1969)

Something / Come Together

U.S.: Apple 2654 (released 6 October 1969)
U.K.: Apple R 5814 (released 31 October 1969)

Let It Be / You Know My Name (Look up the Number)

U.S.: Apple 2764 (released 11 March 1970)
U.K.: Apple R 5833 (released 6 March 1970)

The Long and Winding Road / For You Blue

U.S.: Apple 2832 (released 11 May 1970)

Related Releases

Hey Jude

U.S.: Apple SW 385 (released 26 February 1970)
U.K.: Apple PCS 7184 (released 11 May 1979)

This 1970 U.S. compilation—not released in Britain for almost a decade—marked the first appearance on album of "Don't Let Me Down."

Anthology 3

(2-CD set)
U.S.: Apple 7243 8 34451 2 7 (released 28 October 1996)
U.K.: Apple CDPCSP 729 (released 28 October 1996)

The second CD of this set comprises the following previously unreleased material from the *Let It Be* / *Abbey Road* era, with recording dates:

I've Got a Feeling (23 January 1969)
She Came in through the Bathroom Window (22 January 1969)
Dig a Pony (22 January 1969)
Two of Us (24 January 1969)
For You Blue (25 January 1969)
Teddy Boy (24, 28 January 1969)
Rip It Up / Shake, Rattle, and Roll / Blue Suede Shoes (26 January 1969)
The Long and Winding Road (31 January 1969, miscredited as 26 January 1969)
Oh! Darling (27 January 1969)
All Things Must Pass (25 February 1969)
Mailman, Bring Me No More Blues (29 January 1969)
Get Back (30 January 1969)

Old Brown Shoe (25 February 1969)
Octopus's Garden (26 April 1969)
Maxwell's Silver Hammer (9 July 1969)
Something (25 February 1969)
Come Together (21 July 1969)
Come and Get It (24 July 1969)
Ain't She Sweet (24 July 1969)
Because (1, 4 August 1969)
Let It Be (25 January 1969)
I Me Mine (3 January 1970)
The End (23 July 1969; 5, 7, 8, 15, 18 August 1969; edited into "final chord" from "A Day in the Life," recorded 22 February 1967)

#1: untitled

(prepared 10 March 1969)
Side 1:
Get Back (23 January 1969)
I've Got a Feeling (fragment: 23 January 1969)
Teddy Boy (24 January 1969)
Two of Us (24 January 1969)
Dig a Pony (23 January 1969)
I've Got a Feeling (23 January 1969)
The Long and Winding Road (22 January 1969)
Side 2:
Let It Be (26 January 1969)
Don't Let Me Down (22 January 1969)
For You Blue (25 January 1969)
Get Back (27 January 1969)
The Walk (27 January 1969)

#2: Get Back

(prepared 28 May 1969)
Side 1:
The One after 909 (30 January 1969)
Rocker (22 January 1969)

Save the Last Dance for Me (22 January 1969)
Don't Let Me Down (22 January 1969)
Dig a Pony (23 January 1969)
I've Got a Feeling (23 January 1969)
Get Back (27, 28 January 1969)
Side 2:
For You Blue (25 January 1969)
Teddy Boy (24 January 1969)
Two of Us (24 January 1969)
Maggie Mae (24 January 1969)
Dig It (26 January 1969)
Let It Be (31 January 1969; 30 April 1969)
The Long and Winding Road (31 January 1969)
Get Back reprise (28 January 1969)

#3: Get Back version 2

(prepared 5 January 1970)
Side 1:
The One after 909 (30 January 1969)
Rocker (22 January 1969)
Save the Last Dance for Me (22 January 1969)
Don't Let Me Down (22 January 1969)
Dig a Pony (23 January 1969)
I've Got a Feeling (24 January 1969)
Get Back (27, 28 January 1969)
Let It Be (31 January 1969; 30 April 1969)
Side 2:
For You Blue (25 January 1969)
Two of Us (24 January 1969)
Maggie Mae (24 January 1969)
Dig It (26 January 1969)
The Long and Winding Road (31 January 1969)
I Me Mine (3 January 1970)
Across the Universe (4, 8 February 1968)
Get Back reprise (28 January 1969)

The following recordings were also made during the 1969 sessions for *Let It Be* and *Abbey Road*. Note that only a portion of the Apple sessions from 22 January 1969 onward were officially recorded by Glyn Johns. Other material survives only on the sync-tape operated by the film crew. Alternate takes taped on the same day as the released versions and solo recordings intended for separate release are not listed below.

22 JANUARY 1969	Going up the Country, Dig a Pony, I've Got a Feeling, Don't Let Me Down, Rocker, Save the Last Dance for Me, She Came in through the Bathroom Window
23 JANUARY 1969	Get Back, Blues, Dig a Pony, I've Got a Feeling
24 JANUARY 1969	Two of Us, Teddy Boy, Dig It
25 JANUARY 1969	*untitled jamming,* Two of Us, Bye Bye Love, Let It Be
26 JANUARY 1969	Shake, Rattle, and Roll, Kansas City, Miss Ann, Lawdy Miss Clawdy, Blue Suede Shoes, You Really Got a Hold on Me, Tracks of My Tears, Let It Be, Isn't It a Pity, The Long and Winding Road
27 JANUARY 1969	*untitled jamming,* Oh! Darling, I've Got a Feeling, The Walk
28 JANUARY 1969	Dig a Pony, Get Back, Love Me Do, Don't Let Me Down, I've Got a Feeling, The One after 909, Billy's Song #1, Billy's Song #2, Teddy Boy
29 JANUARY 1969	I Want You (She's So Heavy), The One after 909, Not Fade Away, Mailman Bring Me No More Blues, Teddy Boy, Besame Mucho
31 JANUARY 1969	Lady Madonna
25 FEBRUARY 1969	Old Brown Shoe, All Things Must Pass, Something *(all solo by George Harrison)*
14 APRIL 1969	The Ballad of John and Yoko *(issued on 1969 single)*

16 April 1969	Something
16, 18 April 1969	Old Brown Shoe *(issued on 1969 single)*
30 April 1969	You Know My Name (Look up the Number) *(issued on 1970 single; based on original recording from 1967)*
24 July 1969	Come and Get It *(solo by Paul McCartney)*, Ain't She Sweet

Get Back / Let It Be

Let It Be was the first studio album in rock history to be released after unofficial bootleg editions of the record had already been circulated. Unauthorized LPs featuring Glyn Johns's rejected version of the *Get Back* album were on open sale in California by September 1969—a full seven months before *Let It Be* reached the shops.

The first bootleg was cunningly titled *Kum Back*. It was almost immediately copied by a Los Angeles organization called Lemon Records, whose *Get Back* album purportedly sold more than one hundred thousand copies. The differences between the contents of *Get Back* and the official *Let It Be* have maintained a market ever since for repackagings of the Glyn Johns acetates, first on vinyl and more recently on CD.

The entire soundtrack from the *Let It Be* film was first released on the double LP *Cinelogue: Let It Be* in the early '70s.

Beatles bootlegging entered a new and even more prolific era in 1974, with the release of two double LPs entitled *Sweet Apple Trax*. These sets introduced collectors to the riches of the Nagra tapes that had been left running throughout the Twickenham and Apple sessions in January 1969. For the first time, Beatles fans were able to hear unedited jam sessions, conversations, and rehearsals from the troubled *Let It Be* era.

Despite the fact that many of the Twickenham tapes were virtually unlistenable in artistic terms, their documentary value ensured that there was an audience for any fresh material. The bootleggers duly obliged, with titles like *The Black Album, Twickenham Jams, Watching Rainbows, Vegemite,* and *Her Majesty* appearing in the late '70s and early '80s.

The first major attempt to collate these January 1969 recordings was made by the bootleg label Vigotone, which released *The Get Back*

Journals in 1986. The original eleven-LP package was upgraded as an eight-CD set in the early '90s.

Previously unheard January 1969 material has continued to surface ever since, notably on albums such as *Code Name Russia, All Things Must Pass Part 2,* and several CDs in the series *Songs from the Past, Rockin' Movie Stars,* and *The Let It Be Rehearsals. Unsurpassed Masters Volume 5* unveiled the entire Apple rooftop concert for the first time.

Vigotone followed the CD release of *The Get Back Journals* with *The Get Back Journals 2,* a magnificently packaged CD boxed set accompanied by a glossy booklet that tabulated all the extant Twickenham material.

Another series of boxed sets provided access to all the surviving recordings from the first day of the Twickenham sessions. One CD apiece on the three volumes of Yellow Dog's *The Ultimate Collection* was devoted to these 2 January 1969 recordings. With the two Vigotone boxes, these represent an almost complete tally of the Twickenham tapes.

At the time of writing, the surviving Apple recordings from the last ten days of January 1969 have yet to be collected into a single package. Instead, single-CD selections continue to appear, the most recent (*Jamming with Heather*) featuring a previously uncirculated jam session with Linda Eastman's young daughter, Heather.

In total, around two hundred bootleg LPs and CDs have been released containing officially unreleased material from the January 1969 sessions.

Abbey Road

Comparatively little material has escaped from the sessions that produced *Abbey Road.* This time there was no film crew to document the making of the album and to ensure that outtakes leaked onto the collectors' market. All that has survived from *Abbey Road* are the master tapes of the sessions retained in the EMI vaults, plus a handful of acetates featuring early mixes of the tracks.

The first major leaking of outtakes from this album occurred on the bootleg LP *No. 3 Abbey Road,* which combined a side of McCartney duets with the folksinger Donovan from 1968, with a selection of rough mixes of the *Abbey Road* songs.

The eight tracks included were "Golden Slumbers," "Carry That Weight," "Her Majesty," "You Never Give Me Your Money," "Octopus's

Garden," "Maxwell's Silver Hammer," "Oh! Darling," and "Something." Most of these were virtually identical to the finished recordings, but lacked final orchestral and vocal overdubs. The major exception was "Something," which retained the lengthy instrumental section later trimmed—sensibly, on this evidence—at the final mixing stage.

Subsequent bootlegs have featured only minor, and insignificant, variations on the *No. 3 Abbey Road* material and have effectively been rendered irrelevant by the official release of *Anthology 3*.

BIBLIOGRAPHY

The following books proved invaluable in the research for this book:

Cott, Jonathan, David Dalton, and Ethan Russell. **The Beatles Get Back.** Apple, 1970. *The lavish, if fragile, paperback book included with the original U.K. release of the* Let It Be *LP, which mixes Russell's superb photographs with Cott and Dalton's revealing, but censored, extracts from the January 1969 dialogue.*

Gambaccini, Paul. **Paul McCartney in His Own Words.** Omnibus, 1976. *McCartney's gentle rejoinder to Lennon, also from the pages of* Rolling Stone.

The Get Back Journals II. Vigotone, 1995. *The booklet accompanying the second of Vigotone's bootleg CD boxed sets.*

Harrison, George. **I Me Mine.** Simon and Schuster, 1980. *The ex-Beatle's autobiography, sumptuously presented but only marginally revealing.*

Heylin, Clinton. **Bootleg!** St. Martins Press, 1995. *A comprehensive history of the bootleg industry.*

Lewisohn, Mark. **The Complete Beatles Recording Sessions.** Hamlyn, 1988. *The official history of the EMI studio recordings, based on complete access to the company's archives and master tapes.*

McCabe, Peter, and Robert D. Schonfeld. **John Lennon: For the Record.** Bantam, 1984. *The full transcript of a typically frank 1971 interview.*

Robertson, John. **The Art and Music of John Lennon.** Omnibus, 1990. *A* valuable critique of Lennon's creative output through the Beatles and beyond.

Sulpy, Doug, and Ray Schweighardt. **Drugs, Divorce, and a Slipping Image.** The 910, 1994. *A track-by-track commentary on the January 1969 recordings, assembled with meticulous attention to detail and much intelligence.*

Taylor, Derek. **Fifty Years Adrift.** Genesis Books, 1985. *A lavishly produced autobiography from the Apple insider and Beatles press officer.*

Tobler, John, and Stuart Grundy. **The Record Producers.** St. Martin's Press, 1982. *Includes a rare interview with Glyn Johns about the January 1969 sessions.*

Wenner, Jann. **Lennon Remembers.** Straight Arrow, 1971. *The* Rolling Stone *interview with Lennon from December 1970, filled with fiery rhetoric about the Beatles' final years.*

Copies of the magazines and newspapers *New Musical Express, Rolling Stone, Disc and Music Echo,* the *Times* (London), *The Beatles Book, Melody Maker,* and *Crawdaddy* were also consulted.

INDEX

Note: a **boldface** number indicates the principal discussion of a song; an *italic* number indicates a photograph.

Get Back (album) (cont.)

"I Me Mine" track, 87

"I've Got a Feeling" track, 93

"Let It Be" track, 90

"Long and Winding Road" track, 94

"One after 909" track, 93

postponement of, 64, 72

"Teddy Boy" track, 38

"Two of Us" track, 82

"Get Back"/"Don't Let Me Down" (single), 47, 98, 129

Get Back Journals, The (bootleg albums), 134–35

Get Back Journals 2, 135

"Gimme Some Truth," 17

"Give Peace a Chance," 54, 65

"Glass Onion," 123

"Going up the Country," 133

"Golden Slumbers," 23, 59, **112,** 113

discography, 129, 135

reviewed, 120, 121

Goldstein, Richard, Sgt. Pepper review, 115

"Goodnight," 121, 127

gospel-soul tradition, 88

Grade, Sir Lew (financier), 52

Grundy, Stuart, The Record Producers, 45, 78

H

"Happiness Is a Warm Gun," 106, 127

"Hard to Handle," 92

Harrison, George, viii, 9, 14, 18, 22, 31, 41, 43, 48, 66, 70, 89

assault charge, 30

attitude of, 2, 19, 20, 32, 38, 42, 62

as composer, 11, 12, 19, 24, 28, 29, 64, 69–70, 96, 119, 122–23 (See also under songs of)

contribution to Starr's "Octopus's Garden," 104, 106

Crawdaddy interview, 62

differences with Lennon, 12, 34

differences with McCartney, 11–12, 21, 23, 27, 81–82

Disc interviews, 57, 62, 64, 102

dress on Abbey Road cover, 63

drug bust of, 46

drug use of, 86

Dylan and, 13, 15, 24

enthusiasm for Klein, 44

enthusiasm for Lord of the Rings project, 57

enthusiasm for Preston, 37–38

guitar playing of, 82, 84, 90, 104, 111, 120

hospitalized with tonsillitis, 45

I Me Mine (autobiography), 36, 86

Melody Maker interview, 101

Moog synthesizer of, 103

New Musical Express interview, 69, 101, 102, 106, 110

on Beatles' future, 125

on difficulty of "Because" harmony, 109

on title of "Sun King," 110

opinion of "Across the Universe," 85

opinion of "Come Together," 99, 100

opinion of "Dig a Pony," 83

opinion of Get Back album, 73

opinion of "I Want You," 106–107

opinion of "I've Got a Feeling," 92

opinion of "Let It Be," 88

opinion of live concert idea, 55

opinion of "Maxwell's Silver Hammer," 60, 102

opinion of Starr as composer, 104–105

performs in Plastic Ono Band, 74

private conversation taped with Starr about McCartney, 23–24

produces album for Jackie Lomax, 5

singing of, 112, 116

sitar playing of, 84

songs of, 86–88, 91, 96–97, 100–102, 107–108

suggestions on altering Beatles' image, 20

suggests that McCartney play keyboard, 15

tamboura, playing of, 84

treatment by Lennon and McCartney, 11–12, 24, 96

trip to Greece, 3

walkout of, 32–35, 82, 98

Woodstock visit of, 8, 11

"Hear Me Lord," 19

Helm, Levon, 100

"Help!", 18